Art in Action

Guy Hubbard
Indiana University

Teacher's Manual
First Course

HOLT, RINEHART AND WINSTON

AUSTIN NEW YORK SAN DIEGO CHICAGO TORONTO MONTREAL

Requests for permission to make copies of any part of the work should be mailed to:
Permissions, Coronado Publishers, 1250 Sixth Avenue, San Diego, CA 92101

Printed in the United States of America   ISBN 0-15-770041-0(7)

2 3 4 5 6 7 8 9 0–92 91 90 89

Table of Contents

Introduction

The content of *Art in Action* is built directly on a foundation of art instruction developed by Guy Hubbard. Dr. Hubbard strives to create books for self-contained art classrooms in which teachers may or may not have sufficient preparation in the teaching of art. *Art in Action* represents his latest refinement of this theory. The result is a book that can be successfully used by mature students in upper elementary grades, by average middle and junior high school students, and by high school students with little art background. *Art in Action*, then, can work equally well in a variety of classroom situations. The purpose of the teacher's edition is to present options that will meet these diverse needs.

Art in Action was originally published under the title of *Art: Discovering and Creating*. The goal of this first edition was the full individualization of art instruction. This goal has been retained in *Art in Action*. However, as stated in the previous paragraph, the goal has been expanded to include as many school situations as possible. Thus, those situations in which students are likely to benefit from more guided instruction are also addressed.

The Structure of the Book

The art content is organized into units of lessons based on the familiar art forms of design, drawing, painting, and sculpture. Since printmaking and collage share many qualities, they have been united into a single unit and so have ceramics, crafts, and textiles. The sixth and final unit consists of lessons selected from various areas of art and directs students to solve artistic problems that are primarily creative and expressive. The lessons in each unit generally progress from simpler, more foundational tasks to those that are more complex and expressive. In this way, students can progress through a unit from beginning to end.

The duration of middle, junior, and senior high school art courses varies considerably, however, and only rarely will students have enough time to complete even a single unit from the book. Moreover, art teachers are well aware of the need for adolescents to experience as wide a range of areas within art as time permits. Students in introductory art classes who discover new aptitudes for art or who have their existing interests reinforced are more likely to continue with their art education throughout their elective programs. To help teachers and students make suitable selections within the units, therefore, the lessons are grouped into *unit strands*.

Unit Strands

Each unit consists of two or three strands. The appropriate strand diagram (that is, the diagram representing the unit strand that includes the lesson being completed) is shown in each lesson of the student text. Students will always complete the strands for each unit in consecutive alphabetical order. (That is, upon completion of strand A, a student is instructed to proceed to strand B; upon completion of strand B, a student is instructed to proceed to strand C; and so forth.) Students do, however, have choices about which lessons within a strand to complete. If necessary or desirable, the teacher may make these choices instead. Decisions about the degrees of freedom students should have are best made by each art teacher, since what an individual or a group of students is likely to be able to undertake successfully varies from class to class. Other factors such as time, classroom space, and the availability of art materials will also play a part in this decision.

Using strands is easy once they are clearly introduced. The following step-by-step instructions and diagram for strand E (Unit II) should provide such an introduction.

Strand E: Drawing Methods and Media

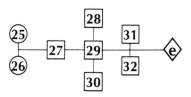

Step 1: Students will begin this strand by choosing and completing either lesson 25 or lesson 26.

Step 2: Students will complete lesson 27.

Step 3: Students will choose and complete lesson 28, lesson 29, or lesson 30.

Step 4: Students will choose and complete either lesson 31 or lesson 32.

Step 5: The diamond-shaped symbol means that students should evaluate their own artwork and proceed to the next strand (in this case, strand F). Note: This symbol appears only in the strand diagram that is given for the last lesson in the strand—in this case, both lesson 31 and lesson 32 would show strand diagrams with this symbol. At this point, students should review the lessons they have completed thus far, noting areas of improvement. They can also evaluate their own work by using the *Learning Outcomes* at the back of the Student Edition.

The Lessons

In order to make the lessons easier to use, a single format is employed. In this way both students and teachers quickly become comfortable using the lessons. Each lesson is clearly written at a level that students should be able to read without difficulty; in a very real sense, each lesson is not only an art lesson, but an exercise in reading comprehension as well.

Each lesson begins with a number followed by a title that provides an indication of content. This is followed by an introductory statement entitled "Observing and Thinking Creatively" that presents information about the art to be studied in that lesson. Next is a set of brief statements entitled "Instructions for Creating Art" which enumerate what the students are to do.

The reproductions to be found within each lesson are included because the foundation of all art studies lies with appropriate visual images. Some of the artworks reproduced within the lessons are by the recognized great artists of the world. Others have been selected from the great civilizations of the past, while still others are works by contemporary artists. Not least, quite a few images are examples of art by adolescents whose work illustrates the intent of a lesson. By means of such a wealth of examples, students are guided through one or more interpretations of a lesson to a clearer understanding of what is expected of them. These pictures have the indispensable function of introducing students to the visual literature of art. Many lessons use visual images to instruct students in art history and the content of criticism, often calling for the students to express their aesthetic feelings about the given art. In addition, all the images in the book contribute informally to the general education of the students by making them familiar with art in various media and with works from different times and places. These images collectively are, in short, a valuable resource for art education.

Goals that are explicitly instructional are served by diagrams of various artistic techniques, pictures of art in progress, and photographs of objects and places. Colored photographs also appear in many lessons to encourage students to observe and interpret both the natural and manmade environment around them.

Each lesson concludes with a list of needed art tools and materials. All these items are of a kind that are found universally in school art rooms, so that no student need be prevented from doing a lesson for want of the proper materials.

Learning Outcomes

Underlying the structure of the units, strands, and lessons is the subject matter of art. The content of the book has been selected from across the range of artistic subject matter. The objectives, or *Learning Outcomes* as they are referred to in the Student Edition, are the heart of the book. The main purpose of the school art program is for students to become educated in the subject of visual art. This means learning information about art as well as demonstrating the understanding that can only come about from the act of handling tools and materials to create art. An education in art also includes coming to value art. Thus, each lesson is based on several learning outcomes selected from these three areas of artistic content.

Anything verbal or visual that a student learns and remembers belongs in the category of *Understanding Art*. This includes words and their definitions, information about artistic techniques, historical information, and also images that a student sees and is expected to remember. The second category is *Creating Art*, and it includes all the learning that occurs when a student is actually producing art. This refers to all the skills a student is to learn, including various safety precautions that must not only be known (Understanding Art) but actually practiced. This category of learning includes most of what is found in traditional art lessons where art production is the primary focus.

Affective valuing is also a necessary part of any art program that claims to be comprehensive. In this book, these learning outcomes fall under the title of *Appreciating Art*. The focus of learning in this area lies with nurturing students' aesthetic values. Performance in this area usually means a visible development of the student's feelings about art through a recognizable increase in the abilities to make choices, orally express preferences, and coherently discuss the qualities he/she considers important in a work of art. It also means being held responsible for giving reasons for a particular point of view. Appreciation objectives in no way mean that student statements need correspond with what a teacher believes or with what is generally held to be the proper assessment of a work. To the contrary, the real task here is to develop a student's ability to reach personal conclusions and justify them. A word of caution is needed with appreciation objectives, however. Most adolescents are developing the abstract thinking skills needed for achieving these objectives, but many of them will not yet have advanced far enough to make complex aesthetic judgments. Moreover, the typical student's experiences with consciously engaging in this kind of thinking is modest compared with other kinds of abstract thinking behavior that receive much more emphasis in the school curriculum. Thus, it is important for you to understand a student's initial reticence during discussions and to work to build a rapport with each student which will enable him or her to confidently express opinions.

Since the study of art consists of content from all three areas of learning, whatever is learned in one area can be expected to affect learning in the other two. For this reason, an improved art vocabulary, together with visual recall of several important artworks is likely to influence a student's aesthetic response to a recently completed artwork by another student in the class. Similarly, the production experience of modeling with clay over an armature is likely to make a student more sensitive to the work involved in the production of a piece of professional sculpture that was executed in the same way.

In sum, the single most important concept in this book is that it is built on a foundation derived from the content of art that, with the help of an art teacher, most adolescent students are likely to be able to learn. Insofar as the content and the structure facilitate student needs, the book will prove to be useful as written. In some circumstances, changes will be needed—as with remediation. On those occasions, an art teacher will be able to do this more easily by modifying the content than by having to start from the beginning.

Evaluation

Evaluation in art presents difficulties that separate it from evaluation in other subjects. On the other hand, much of the art that can be learned may be evaluated in much the same way as in other subjects. The first step to managing the evaluation task is to be found in the statements listed at the end of the Student Edition under *Learning Outcomes*. Each of these statements either establishes what a student should have learned or calls for the student to respond in such a way that he or she shows what has been learned. If student performance is compared with these learning outcome statements, then evaluation is practical. For example, when students are asked to paint with various thicknesses of transparent watercolor, the finished painting will provide the needed information.

Similar comparisons can be made for knowledge about art and also for appreciating art. The methods used for determining achievement in these two areas are likely to include such things as having students, either orally or in writing, use particular words correctly in context or recognize the period of a painting. Also, they might either describe or draw an object that was to have been remembered. Learning in the area of appreciation usually calls for some kind of oral or written explanation that throws light on why students made a particular decision.

Art vocabulary is relatively easy to evaluate. It is apparent when a student defines a word accurately, spells it correctly, and uses it properly in context. Similarly, learning outcomes relative to historical knowledge as well as to skill with artistic techniques are relatively simple to evaluate. Students either know it or can do it to a level that is reasonable for adolescents—or they cannot. Degrees of knowledge and skillfulness are more difficult to assess, but setting standards for minimal performance normally does not present great difficulty.

Evaluation problems escalate dramatically when the task goes beyond skills and facts. If a student satisfies the stated criteria, then he or she has succeeded with that part of the lesson—but only at a minimal level. Evaluative decisions beyond this minimal level can only be made by teachers in the classroom. Only they have the knowledge and understanding to make more complete judgements about student work. For example, one student who has barely met the criteria for a given lesson may deserve special credit if he or she has a handicap that makes such an achievement difficult. In contrast, another student might far exceed the minimal objective and yet be credited with only marginal success because he or she has natural talent but did not apply it during the lesson. The objectives referred to in the learning outcomes, therefore, are intended only to point toward a desired direction. Only the art teacher is competent from that time on to judge the quality of a given performance by an individual student or an entire class.

Several other references to evaluation need to be made. The first has to do with learning outcomes that a teacher believes need attention but which are not mentioned in the book. Although lists of learning outcomes for each lesson are appropriate for the lesson as written, a teacher may see the need for some other objective to be achieved from that activity. In this case, it should be added or substituted in the Student Edition so students know what they are expected to learn.

Another departure from the book will occur when students show that they have learned something of value that was not asked for. For example, a student may use words in a particularly expressive way, or render gradations of curved forms in an especially sensitive way. It would be unfair to a student for such unexpected performance to be disregarded just because that particular outcome was not identified in the lesson. Evaluation at its best should give credit for what is learned, regardless of whether it was specified or whether it happens unexpectedly.

The need for evaluation also provides unique opportunities for enhancing student learning. During the original field testing of the program, and on several occasions since, students have taken turns using the learning outcomes to evaluate the work of their classmates. As long as the statements of what was to be learned are clearly stated, students make excellent evaluations. Moreover, the act of evaluating seems to compel student evaluators to master the content of the lesson more than they would when evaluated by their teachers. The student whose work was being evaluated, moreover, also tended to check more carefully that he or she had done everything that was expected before submitting the work for evaluation. The only problem with this strategy lies in the tendency for some student evaluations to be unnecessarily harsh; thus, the teacher must become a tempering influence. The benefits of peer evaluation are significant, however.

The learning outcomes are also useful tools for students to use to evaluate themselves. The individ-ualized nature of the program naturally calls for some measure of self-evaluation. By referring to the learning outcomes upon completion of every lesson, students can actually check their own progress and recognize the areas that require additional work. The learning outcomes, then, are inherently useful for the three types of evaluation: teacher, peer, and self.

Use of Critical Thinking Skills

The format of each lesson in *Art in Action* has been developed to elicit the use of critical thinking skills combined with creative observation. The title at the beginning of each lesson, *Observing and Thinking Creatively*, implies the significance of these skills in the process of art learning. The text for the lessons has been written inductively in order to relate to students' experiences, involve their active participation, and encourage higher levels of thinking.

Students are often asked to respond to the visual images in the lesson. These images fall into four different categories: artwork by master artists, representative students' artwork, photographs, or illustrations of methods and techniques. Captions that provide specific information about the artists, art styles, media, and techniques are included for famous works of art. The captions also encourage students to study the visuals to observe particular art elements and principles that make them noteworthy.

Following the visuals, specific step-by-step instructions guide students through the process of art production. These instructions are written so that most students can work independently, allowing the teacher time to meet with individual students or attend to other tasks. Further individualization is possible if students follow the art strand at the end of each lesson, enabling them to move ahead at their own pace. Before proceeding to the next lesson, students are encouraged to evaluate their work using the *Learning Outcomes* at the back of the Student Edition. (See the preceding discussion of *Learning Outcomes* for a complete description). As previously stated, the *Learning Outcomes* can function as a means for self-, peer-, and teacher evaluation. An *Art Evaluation Record Sheet* on page xii has been included for this purpose. The *Learning Outcomes* have been written to encourage the use of higher level thinking skills and are based on Benjamin Bloom's *Taxonomy of Education Objectives*.

Learning Outcomes Correlated to Critical Thinking Skills

The Learning Outcomes for each lesson are grouped in a special section at the back of each student book. They are explained in detail on pages vi and vii of the Teacher's Manual. Students and teachers may refer to the Learning Outcomes after each lesson and use them as the criteria for evaluating art learning. The questions and statements included in the *Learning Outcomes* are based on the use of critical thinking skills as explained by Benjamin Bloom and his co-writers in *A Taxonomy of Educational Objectives in the Cognitive Domain*. The charts on the next few pages show the relationship between the *Learning Outcomes* and the six levels of thinking—knowledge, comprehension, application, analysis, synthesis, and evaluation.

KNOWLEDGE Recall information learned in a similar form

Behaviorial Terms Indicating Knowledge:

list	repeat
define	quote
state	spell
name	recite
select	label
locate	identify
observe	memorize
show	match

Sample Learning Outcomes (Student Edition):

List art materials other than pencils that are good for drawing.
(Lesson 25; page 234)

Define *unity* in art.
(Lesson 27; page 234)

Name some techniques for unifying a still life picture.
(Lesson 45; page 237)

Learning Outcomes Requiring Use of Knowledge:*

1.1, 2.1, 3.1, 4.1, 5.1, 6.1, 6.2, 8.1, 9.1, 10.1, 10.2, 13.1, 13.2, 14.1, 15.1, 16.1, 19.1, 19.4, 20.1, 20.2, 21.2, 22.1, 23.2, 25.1, 26.1, 27.1, 27.2, 28.1, 30.1, 33.1, 34.1, 35.1, 38.1, 39.2, 40.1, 41.1, 41.2, 44.1, 44.2, 45.1, 45.2, 47.1, 48.2, 49.1, 50.1, 51.1, 52.1, 53.1, 56.1, 56.2, 57.1, 58.2, 61.1, 62.1, 63.1, 64.1, 66.1, 67.1, 68.1, 68.2, 72.1, 72.2, 76.1, 77.1, 78.1, 79.2, 80.1, 80.2, 81.1, 82.1, 82.2, 83.1, 84.1, 85.1, 87.1, 88.1, 89.1, 90.1, 93.1, 94.1, 94.2, 95.2

Teacher's Manual:**

3, 11, 13, 21, 22, 29, 33, 39, 44, 48, 53, 54, 55, 63, 66, 77, 80, 84, 85, 87

COMPREHENSION Understand and interpret information learned in a different form

Behavioral Terms Indicating Comprehension:

describe	generalize
reword	paraphrase
render	summarize
convert	translate
tell	infer
expand	outline
explain	project
specify	calculate

Sample Learning Outcomes (Student Edition):

Describe the art style of the Impressionist painters.
(Lesson 48; page 238)

Tell what you learned through the process of making abstract art.
(Lesson 54; page 239)

Explain how Theo van Doesberg made an abstract picture of a cow.
(Lesson 54; page 239)

Learning Outcomes Requiring Use of Comprehension:*

1.1, 1.5, 3.3, 4.2, 6.3, 6.4, 7.1, 7.4, 9.2, 10.1, 10.2, 10.3, 11.1, 12.1, 12.3, 15.1, 17.1, 18.1, 18.2, 19.2, 21.1, 23.1, 24.1, 26.5, 28.2, 29.1, 31.1, 32.1, 33.2, 34.3, 36.1, 37.1, 38.2, 39.1, 40.2, 42.1, 42.2, 43.1, 46.1, 48.1, 53.2, 54.1, 54.5, 55.1, 56.4, 57.3, 57.4, 58.1, 58.2, 59.1, 60.1, 62.2, 65.1, 65.3, 67.2, 69.1, 70.1, 71.1, 73.1, 74.1, 75.1, 79.1, 83.2, 84.2, 86.1, 90.4, 91.1, 92.1, 95.1

Teacher's Manual:**

7, 8, 9, 16, 19, 22, 23, 28, 30, 34, 36, 38, 40, 42, 44, 45, 52, 54, 55, 58, 60, 64, 65, 74, 79, 81

Student Edition
 *The first number of the *Learning Outcomes* represents the lesson number, the second refers to a specific question.
Teacher's Manual
 **Numbers refer to lesson numbers. Thinking skills are found under "Planning Ahead" and "Helpful Teaching Hints."

Learning Outcomes
Correlated to Critical Thinking Skills
(Continued)

APPLICATION	ANALYSIS
Use information learned to relate or apply ideas to new or unusual situations	**Examine and break information down into its component parts and identify its unique characteristics**

Behavioral Terms Indicating Application:

apply	transfer
utilize	employ
change	manipulate
sketch	exercise
produce	develop
show	mobilize
dramatize	solve
demonstrate	relate

Behavioral Terms Indicating Analysis:

examine	separate
analyze	select
categorize	inspect
classify	scrutinize
simplify	survey
compare	search
diagram	experiment
dissect	illustrate

Sample Learning Outcomes (Student Edition):

Describe how you designed your poster to catch people's attention.
(Lesson 17; page 233)

Did you practice drawing textures?
(Lesson 22; page 234)

Tell how you made some objects look closer and others far away.
(Lesson 30; page 235)

Sample Learning Outcomes (Student Edition):

What mood or feeling do you get from Frederic Clay Bartlett's *Blue Rafters* in the lesson?
(Lesson 45; page 237)

Which parts of your design did you emphasize? What colors did you repeat?
(Lesson 52; page 238)

Explain how your two artworks are different. Point out specific contrasts in shape, color, texture, size, details, expressions, and so on.
(Lesson 92; page 244)

Learning Outcomes Requiring Use of Application:*

1.2, 1.3, 2.2, 3.2, 3.3, 4.2, 5.2, 7.2, 8.2, 9.3, 10.3, 11.2, 12.2, 12.3, 13.3, 15.2, 17.2, 18.3, 19.3, 19.4, 20.3, 20.4, 21.3, 21.4, 22.2, 22.3, 23.3, 24.2, 25.2, 26.2, 26.4, 27.3, 27.4, 28.3, 29.2, 29.3, 30.2, 30.3, 30.4, 31.2, 32.2, 33.3, 34.2, 37.2, 37.3, 38.3, 39.3, 40.3, 41.3, 41.4, 42.3, 43.2, 44.3, 45.3, 46.2, 47.2, 47.3, 48.3, 49.3, 50.2, 51.2, 51.3, 52.2, 52.3, 53.3, 54.2, 55.2, 56.3, 57.2, 58.3, 59.2, 60.2, 61.2, 62.3, 63.2, 64.2, 65.2, 66.2, 67.3, 68.3, 69.2, 70.2, 71.2, 72.3, 73.2, 74.2, 75.2, 76.2, 77.2, 78.2, 79.3, 80.3, 81.2, 82.3, 84.3, 85.2, 86.2, 87.2, 88.2, 89.2, 90.2, 91.2, 92.2, 93.2, 94.3, 95.3

Teacher's Manual:**

3, 5, 12, 16, 19, 20, 22, 25, 30, 34, 35, 45, 46, 48, 50, 53, 73, 82, 83, 91, 93

Learning Outcomes Requiring Use of Analysis:*

1.3, 2.4, 3.5, 4.3, 5.3, 6.3, 7.4, 8.2, 9.5, 10.3, 11.2, 11.4, 15.4, 18.2, 18.4, 19.5, 20.5, 22.3, 22.4, 23.5, 24.4, 27.5, 29.4, 30.5, 31.4, 34.4, 34.5, 35.4, 37.4, 39.3, 39.4, 40.4, 42.5, 47.4, 48.4, 49.5, 50.5, 54.4, 55.5, 56.3, 56.5, 57.5, 58.4, 59.4, 60.4, 60.5, 61.4, 62.5, 63.4, 65.4, 66.4, 67.5, 69.4, 71.5, 73.5, 75.4, 76.4, 80.5, 81.5, 82.5, 83.4, 84.5, 85.4, 86.5, 87.5, 88.4, 89.4, 92.3, 92.4, 93.5, 94.5

Teacher's Manual:**

1, 2, 14, 24, 26, 35, 37, 39, 41, 45, 46, 48, 50, 51, 53, 57, 68, 69, 70

Student Edition
  *The first number of the *Learning Outcomes* represents the lesson number, the second refers to a specific question.
Teacher's Manual
  **Numbers refer to lesson numbers. Thinking skills are found under "Planning Ahead" and "Helpful Teaching Hints."

SYNTHESIS
Communicate, generate, or develop something new and original from what is learned

Behavioral Terms Indicating Synthesis:

unify	develop
combine	design
compose	originate
create	produce
form	generate
assemble	arrange
reorganize	invent
construct	imagine

Sample Learning Outcomes (Student Edition):

Did you make a unified design using colors, shapes, and lines? Describe what you did to create unity.
(Lesson 41; page 237)

Describe how you used different kinds of lines to create a shape or pattern in your picture.
(Lesson 43; page 237)

How do you create a center of interest?
(Lesson 76; page 242)

Learning Outcomes Requiring Use of Synthesis:*

1.2, 1.3, 2.2, 3.2, 3.3, 3.4, 5.2, 7.3, 8.3, 9.4, 10.4, 13.4, 14.2, 15.2, 15.3, 16.2, 17.2, 17.3, 20.4, 22.3, 23.4, 24.2, 24.3, 25.3, 26.3, 26.4, 27.4, 28.4, 29.3, 30.4, 31.3, 31.5, 32.3, 33.4, 35.2, 35.3, 36.2, 36.3, 41.4, 42.4, 42.5, 43.3, 43.4, 44.4, 44.5, 45.4, 46.3, 46.4, 46.5, 49.4, 50.2, 50.3, 51.2, 51.4, 52.2, 53.4, 54.3, 55.3, 55.4, 59.4, 60.3, 61.3, 63.3, 64.3, 64.4, 65.3, 66.3, 67.4, 68.4, 68.5, 69.3, 70.3, 71.3, 71.4, 72.4, 72.5, 73.2, 74.3, 74.4, 75.3, 76.3, 77.3, 78.3, 79.4, 80.4, 81.3, 81.4, 82.4, 83.3, 84.4, 85.3, 86.3, 87.3, 88.2, 88.3, 89.3, 90.3, 91.3, 92.3, 93.3, 94.4, 95.4

Teacher's Manual:**

1, 21, 22, 34, 35, 46, 48, 50, 53, 55, 63, 73, 74, 75, 81, 82, 83, 87, 92, 94

EVALUATION
Make judgments and evaluate something based on either external or internal conditions or criteria

Behavioral Terms Indicating Evaluation:

evaluate	estimate
judge	measure
value	recommend
decide	assess
determine	criticize
rate	justify
appraise	grade
rank	discriminate

Sample Learning Outcomes (Student Edition):

Tell which of the four word pictures you designed is the best and explain why.
(Lesson 16; page 233)

Tell what you like about the way Rembrandt drew the elephant in this lesson.
(Lesson 21; page 234)

Compare the two artists' pictures in the lesson. Tell which picture you prefer and why.
(Lesson 28; page 235)

Learning Outcomes Requiring Use of Evaluation:*

1.4, 1.5, 2.3, 2.5, 3.5, 4.3, 5.4, 6.5, 8.4, 9.5, 10.5, 11.4, 12.4, 13.5, 14.3, 15.4, 16.3, 17.4, 18.5, 19.4, 20.4, 21.5, 22.4, 23.5, 24.4, 25.4, 27.5, 28.5, 29.4, 30.5, 32.4, 33.5, 34.4, 36.4, 37.4, 38.5, 39.5, 40.1, 40.5, 41.5, 45.5, 47.4, 48.4, 49.5, 50.5, 51.5, 53.5, 55.5, 56.5, 58.4, 59.4, 60.5, 61.4, 62.4, 63.4, 64.5, 66.5, 67.5, 69.4, 69.5, 70.4, 71.5, 73.4, 75.4, 76.5, 77.4, 78.4, 80.5, 81.5, 82.5, 83.4, 84.5, 86.4, 87.5, 89.4, 91.4, 92.4, 93.4, 93.5

Teacher's Manual:**

1, 2, 13, 14, 15, 17, 18, 35, 41, 42, 46, 49, 50, 53, 55, 57, 61, 85, 88, 91, 93

Student Edition
 *The first number of the *Learning Outcomes* represents the lesson number, the second refers to a specific question.
Teacher's Manual
 **Numbers refer to lesson numbers. Thinking skills are found under "Planning Ahead" and "Helpful Teaching Hints."

Art Evaluation Record Sheet

Name: _____ **Date:** _____

Lesson Number: _____

Strand Identification (if used): _____

Instructions: Refer to the *Learning Outcomes* section (at the back of your book) which corresponds to the lesson you are evaluating. Use the blanks below to answer the questions listed for the lesson.

Understanding Art: _____

_____

_____

_____

_____

_____

_____

Creating Art: _____

_____

_____

_____

_____

_____

_____

_____

_____

_____

_____

_____

Appreciating Art: _____

_____

_____

_____

_____

_____

_____

_____

How to Do It: Art Media, Materials, and Techniques

A special section entitled *How to Do It* appears at the back of the Student Edition. The purpose of this section is to provide additional information on the use of art tools and materials, media, and techniques. It includes specific directions for how to do certain activities referred to in the lessons, such as mixing colors, preparing clay, or making papier-mâché. Key italicized words marked with asterisks within the lessons refer students to the *How to Do It* section for further information. In addition to providing more extensive coverage of methods, media, and art materials, large photographs and illustrations enhance visual learning of such processes. Safety precautions for hazardous tools or materials are also featured throughout the section where necessary.

Students and teachers are encouraged to become familiar with the contents of this section, not only for completing art lessons within the text, but also because the knowledge gained in this section enables students to improve their art skills and become more self-sufficient. The benefits for the teacher are also quite substantial. As students become more independent in referring to this section, they are less likely to depend on the teacher to provide the information for them.

The Glossary

Throughout the book, particular words and skills recur that students need to learn. Important words are identified in heavy type and are defined in the Glossary at the end of the Student Edition. All such words are defined in the text on the first occasion they are used. Since most students will do only a portion of the total number of lessons, they are also defined in the Glossary.

Artists' Reference and Index

A complete *Artists' Reference* and *Index* are included at the end of the Student Edition. The *Artists' Reference* provides a list of all reproductions of major artworks by master artists included in the book.

Book Strands

Book strands offer unique opportunities for individualization of art education to occur. There are seventeen book strands identified by names such as "Enjoying Color" and "Ideas from Other Cultures." Students will enjoy being able to choose a strand with a title they find interesting. Likewise, students will appreciate being able to identify those other lessons that have themes and concepts relevant to a lesson they particularly enjoyed. In anticipation of this desire, each lesson outline in this teacher's edition is followed by a book strand that includes the lesson. This makes it easy for you to direct interested students on a course of study they will enjoy.

Following is a short description of each book strand, including the philosophy behind its conception. Using the book strands is just like using the unit strands; see pages v and vi for these instructions.

Strand 1: Thinking with Contours
Students are first introduced to opposite ways in which contours separate objects from their surroundings. Step Two directs them to varied artistic applications of contours, with the focus on outer edges. Step Three offers students opportunities to explore external contours in greater depth or to apply this knowledge to drawings of people.

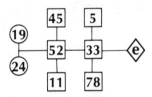

Strand 2: Abstract Puzzles
Abstraction is often easier to introduce as design than as a picture, and this is done at Step One with both two and three dimensions. Step Two continues this exploration of two- and three-dimensional abstraction with decorated plaster casting and stitchery design. The strand ends with two abstractions that derive from the sound of music and from the shapes of objects.

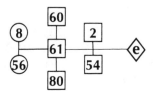

Strand 3: Artistic Visions
This strand invites students to learn about the artistic visions of artists. The paintings of Henri Matisse are colorful and spontaneous and provide a non-threatening introduction to the topic. Step Two provides three opportunities for students to develop their artistic visions while also becoming informed about the different media through which artists express themselves. The strand ends with lessons that focus on a great artist and a great cultural tradition.

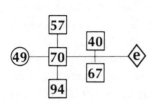

Strand 4: Art with Flat Planes
Step One opens with an exercise on observing and rendering flat surfaces and the contours that define them. In Step Two, students work directly with plane surfaces at construction tasks. Step Three carries the study of planes further by means of clay sculpture, slab pottery, and a more elaborate assignment using cardboard.

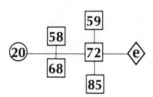

Strand 5: Faces and Feelings
The strand opens with lessons about proportions and expressions on faces, especially eyes. Step Two focuses on feelings that are expressed on faces through the kind of distortion found in comic strip art. The strand ends with several different opportunities for showing feelings on people's faces.

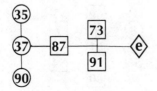

Strand 6: Enjoying Color
A lesson on tissue collage opens this exploration of color in art. In Step Two, experiences in the use of crayon etching and oil pastels are highlighted. Last of all, the strand advances to two contrasting lessons, the first on the colorful painting style of the Impressionists and the other on the equally colorful art of Mexican nearikas.

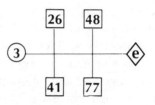

Strand 7: Exploring Textures
Since textures can be either real or rendered, the strand opens with a choice between a drawing and a textile collage. Step Two provides opportunities for working with textures in printmaking, pottery decoration, and woven textiles. The concluding step requires students to select and carve textures ranging from the extremes of roughness to those of smoothness.

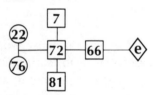

Strand 8: Studying Lines
The choices for Step One include drawing and painting lessons that focus on creating with lines. In Step Two, crayon etching and stitchery are tied to and, in fact, expand on the concept of line. The strand ends with the more disciplined application of line found in representational drawing and calligraphy.

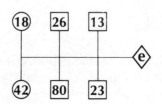

Strand 9: Composing Pictures and Designs
This strand draws attention to composition as artistic problem solving, first by means of collage or letter forms. Step Two consists of lessons where students may complete a composition from a larger visual field. The strand ends with lessons on advertising and sculptural composition.

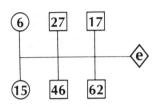

Strand 10: Ideas from Other Cultures
Students can add considerably to their knowledge and expressiveness by studying the art of other cultures. Steps One and Two introduce the students to four very different artistic traditions. Step Three challenges the students to apply what they have learned to creating art that is based on work from other cultures while still remaining uniquely their own.

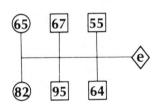

Strand 11: Imagineering
This strand is designed to encourage artistic imagination. At Step One, students have an opportunity to work in an unrestrained way with monoprints and oil pastels. The Step Two choices are designed to give students opportunities to choose among three very different imaginative experiences. The last step takes students further by having them produce two contrasting works.

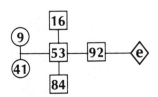

Strand 12: The Look of Distance
This strand is intended to help overcome the problems students have with conveying the illusion of depth on a flat surface. The first two choices in Step One are taken from the sequence of lessons in Unit II that introduce simple perspective techniques. The choices in Step Two address similar tasks, but ask students to use transparent or opaque paint. Step Three offers students an opportunity to use what they have learned by producing a picture or an illustration.

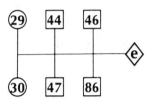

Strand 13: Artistic Surprises
Good art often happens when least expected, and that is what is being encouraged in the first step of this strand. In this step, students search for ideas in chance designs. In Step Two, students are asked for more deliberate work that is also likely to lead to surprising results. The last step invites students to show images that are surprising and, quite probably, humorous.

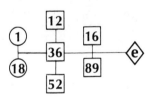

Strand 14: From Observation to Imagination
The foundation of art lies in observation, which is where this strand begins. Step Two asks students to draw what they have seen and remembered, while the lessons in Step Three ask them to take images they have remembered and use them imaginatively.

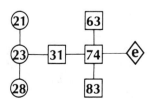

Strand 15: All About People
Step One asks students to draw the human body in proportion. At Step Two they are encouraged to be more spontaneous in the ways they use people. Step Three gives students the opportunity to extend their expressiveness about people still further by means of a sports picture or an abstract portrait.

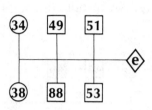

Strand 16: Being a Designer
Step One introduces students to two types of problems that designers solve when creating art for everyday life. Steps Two and Three continue this theme with more complex tasks for lettering and symbol design, and, lastly, for jewelry, pottery, and architecture.

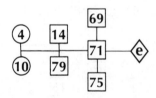

Strand 17: The Quest for Self-Expression
Step One introduces the students to alternative drawing media and artistic styles. Step Two expands on media and styles, while also focusing on observation and visual memory. Finally, the students choose between two open-ended lessons that test their willingness to search for fresh ways of expressing themselves.

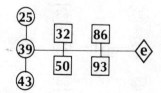

Strand 18: Seeing Shapes
The choices for Step One focus on the importance of shape in design using colored or black and white paper. In Step Two, shapes can be created with lines or without lines. The strand ends with a choice of recognizing shape as a part of abstract art or sculpture.

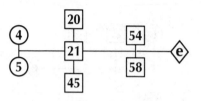

Strand 19: Form in Art
The opening strand choices allow for two very different approaches to learning about form—making a collage of objects or a contour drawing. In Step Two, students continue working with three-dimensional form in sculpture, or create the illusion of form in objects or the human body with shading and line. The final step explores form in three different three-dimensional media.

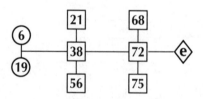

Strand 20: Sizing Up Relationships
This strand focuses on the value of proportion in creating balanced yet varied artwork. Proportions of negative to positive space or of letter designs are choices in Step One. Step Two focuses on exaggerated proportions of perspective and a study of facial proportions. Step Three offers more opportunity to work with proportions of the human form or to continue examining spatial and linear proportions in architecture.

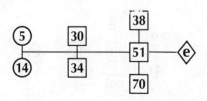

Strand 21: Artists and Art Styles

This strand is designed to chronologically expose the student to several different art styles and famous artists. Step One includes choices among ancient Oriental brush painting, stylized African art, or symbolic art of the American Indian. The examining style of Leonardo da Vinci, the larger-than-life style of Mexican art, or the innovative use of color by the Impressionists are options in Step Two. The strand ends with the choices of either modern abstract art or Pop art.

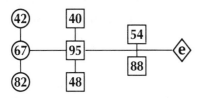

Strand 22: Recognizing Rhythm

In Step One the student can identify the concept of rhythm of repeated design elements by working with the familiar rhythm of music. The repetition of line, shape or color to create rhythm are expanded in the lesson choices in Step Two. Finally, the brushwork of Oriental art or the colorful patterned style of Matisse provide outstanding examples of rhythm to reinforce the students' understanding of this design principle.

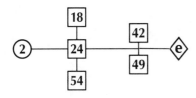

Strand 23: A Sense of Motion

In the first lesson of this strand, the student creates a balanced design in which line, shape, and color move the viewer's eye throughout the artwork. Step Two includes three painting lessons dealing with very different subject matter. Here the importance of movement within the artwork, whether by line, pattern, color or shape is stressed also. In Step Three, movement is emphasized by creating a yarn design or by making a design using symbolism.

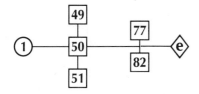

Applying the Strand Concept

As you can see, book strands and unit strands offer remarkable individualization possibilities. However, because of the immaturity or inexperience of their students, teachers may think it wise to restrict student choices to a few strands. Occasionally, though, a class may be mature enough to be given the freedom to select any strand—unit or book—and choose any pathway through it. In fact, the experience gained during the two years of field testing through which these books originally went indicates that a larger proportion of students than would have been thought possible respond favorably to being responsible for their own education in this way. Furthermore, experience shows that, with a curriculum based on individualization, students who work slowly no longer experience pressure to keep pace with other students in the class, while the faster and generally more capable students are not frustrated by having to wait for the rest of the class to complete an assignment. Another outcome of full individualization, unexpected but desirable, is that the quantity of tools and materials needed to operate an art program declines considerably because of the dispersal of need and the variable speed of student production. Teachers should realize one thing about full individualization, however. With such a program it becomes necessary to maintain some form of written evaluation with the students in order to make record-keeping manageable. An example of such an evaluation form is depicted on page 52, but teachers should choose any format with which they are comfortable.

Postscript

The remainder of this Teacher's Edition provides useful information about the units and the concepts to be mastered in the lessons that make up the units, together with ideas and book references for enriching and supplementing instruction. A scope and sequence chart and a supplies chart showing art materials needed throughout the course are also included.

Art In Action: Scope and Sequence (First Course)

I. Elements of Art

Line	5, 22-24, 31, 43-47, 50, 59, 60, 65, 74, 76, 85, 87, 91, 95-98, 106, 110, 116, 117, 119, 121, 125, 146, 147, 151, 192, 198, 202, 204, 207
Shape	5-7, 9, 11, 13-16, 18-19, 22-24, 29, 32-33, 36, 37, 44-45, 54, 56-58, 68, 69, 76, 87, 98, 102-103, 113, 116-121, 125, 127, 132-145, 148-149, 180, 202, 209, 210
Form	5, 6, 8, 46, 48, 84, 85, 91, 118, 127, 129, 131-135, 137-139, 144-145, 148-151, 162-163, 165, 170-171, 189
Space	5-9, 15, 32, 41, 45, 56-57, 62-63, 96, 127, 132, 148, 217
Texture	5-6, 8-10, 16, 18-19, 22-23, 52-54, 58-59, 91, 103, 127, 139, 148, 153, 154, 158, 172-173, 180, 208
Color	3, 5-13, 16, 24-25, 37, 40-41, 48, 54, 60-61, 64, 72, 76, 91, 93-95, 97, 99-101, 103, 105-111, 113, 119, 121, 125, 170, 173, 177, 186, 191, 199, 204, 207, 209, 210, 217
Value	3, 5, 48-50, 53, 68-69, 76, 91, 93-94, 101, 106, 117

II. Principles of Art

Balance	5, 7, 14-15, 21, 25, 32, 41, 76-77, 79, 103, 107, 125, 129, 135, 154-155, 174, 184, 186, 214, 217
Variety	5, 7, 11, 16-17, 19, 23, 25, 27, 50, 52, 57, 59, 93, 101, 107, 133, 136-137, 149, 172-173, 180-181, 183
Rhythm	5, 8-9, 21, 23, 24, 27, 45, 47, 57, 96-97, 110, 111, 117, 125, 184, 190, 200
Movement	5, 6-7, 8, 9, 41, 46, 58, 60, 65, 91, 93, 96-97, 104, 110-111, 112-113, 114-115, 148, 174, 184, 200, 217
Emphasis	5, 7, 41, 44, 58, 60, 64, 95, 97, 104, 105, 110, 112, 113, 114, 115, 173, 204-205, 214
Proportion	14-15, 32, 56-57, 64-65, 66-67, 68-69, 74-77, 79, 80-85, 91, 105, 115, 156-158
Unity	5, 6-7, 8-9, 13, 37, 38, 41, 61, 63, 95, 103, 117, 123, 129, 180, 209, 210

III. Creative Expression Using Various Media and Materials

Drawing: pencil	44-51, 64-71, 74-87, 90-91, 102-105, 115-121, 124, 186
charcoal	59, 87, 90
ink	11, 35, 45, 73, 87, 90, 99, 137, 139, 191, 197, 199, 207
chalk	14-15, 64-65, 91
crayon	45, 59, 71, 73, 81, 87, 91, 93
oil pastel	61, 71, 73, 81, 87, 90, 191, 197, 199, 209
colored marker	35, 37, 45, 71, 73, 81, 95, 137, 158, 169, 191, 197, 199, 201, 207
Painting: watercolor	94-95, 98-99, 100-101, 114-115
tempera	40, 106-107, 114-117, 145
other	93, 96-99, 102-105, 108-109, 110-111, 112-113, 116-121, 124, 174-175, 190-191, 193, 196-197, 205-209, 212-213
Printmaking: natural objects	18-19, 26-27
man-made objects	20-21, 28-29
linoleum blocks	28-29
one-time	22-23
string	24-25
vegetables	26-27
other	203
Sculpture: modeling	143-147, 154-159, 194-195
carving	27-29, 147-149, 151, 186, 195, 211
constructing	128-137, 152-155, 168-169

VII. Related Subject Areas (Cont'd)	
Social Studies	14, 20, 26, 74, 88, 96, 108-112, 125, 127, 132, 140, 144, 146, 150-151, 159, 161, 167, 174, 181, 184, 186, 187, 192, 204, 212, 214-217
Mathematics	50, 68, 112, 116-117
Science	16, 54, 55, 88, 98, 99, 127, 168, 212
Music	8-9, 46, 70, 206
Industrial Arts	20-21, 56, 112-113, 116-117, 134
Creative Arts	14, 104, 108, 112, 118, 159, 187, 194, 195, 196, 206

VIII. Aesthetic Valuing Using Critical Thinking Skills

Knowledge	6, 8, 10, 12, 14, 18, 20, 22, 24, 26, 28, 30, 34, 37, 38, 40, 41, 43, 45, 46, 48, 50, 52, 54, 56, 58, 60, 62, 64, 66, 68-70, 72, 74, 77, 78, 80, 82, 84, 86, 87, 88, 90, 93, 94, 95-98, 100, 102, 104, 106, 108-113, 116, 118, 120, 122, 125, 127, 128, 130, 132-136, 138, 140, 142-144, 146, 148-152, 154, 156, 159, 162, 164, 166, 168, 170, 172, 174, 176, 178, 180-182, 184, 186, 189, 192, 195, 196, 198, 200, 204, 207, 208, 209, 211, 213, 214, 216, 217
Comprehension	8, 11, 12, 16, 17, 19, 20, 25, 26, 28, 31, 32, 36, 38, 41, 43-48, 50, 52-54, 56, 58, 60, 62, 64, 66, 69, 70, 74-78, 81, 84, 86, 87, 90, 93-95, 97, 98, 100, 102, 106, 108-110, 112-114, 116, 118, 120, 121-123, 125, 127, 130, 133, 134, 140, 142, 144, 148, 150, 151, 154, 159, 164, 166, 168, 173, 176, 178, 179, 181, 186, 187, 189-192, 196-198, 200, 202, 204, 208-211, 216-217

VIII. Aesthetic Valuing Using Critical Thinking Skills (Cont'd)

Application	6-8, 10, 13-15, 20, 22-29, 31, 38, 40, 41, 43, 45-49, 51, 53, 56-58, 61, 62, 65-70, 73-79, 82-86, 90, 91, 93-97, 99, 101-111, 115-121, 124, 127, 132, 135-137, 139-141, 143-145, 147, 149, 151, 158, 162, 163, 165, 173, 174, 180, 181-183, 198-199, 204, 207-210, 213, 214, 216
Analysis	6, 9, 11, 17, 19, 21-23, 25, 27, 29, 31, 33, 35-38, 43-45, 49, 51-53, 55, 59-62, 67, 70, 72, 74-79, 81, 85-88, 91, 93-95, 98, 99, 103, 104, 107, 109-115, 117, 120-125, 131, 135, 137, 139, 146-149, 152, 155, 158, 164, 169, 173, 174, 179, 186, 193, 196-198, 201-206, 208, 210, 211, 214, 217
Synthesis	6, 7, 9, 10, 16-19, 21, 24, 27-30, 33, 34, 36-38, 40, 43, 45, 51, 55-57, 59, 61, 63, 67, 69, 71-73, 75, 77-80, 83, 85-87, 90, 91, 93-95, 97, 99, 101, 103-105, 107, 109, 111-113, 115, 117-119, 121, 127-132, 134-140, 143, 145-149, 151-154, 156, 158, 159, 161, 163-173, 175, 176, 178, 179, 185-187, 189-194, 196, 198-200, 202, 204, 205, 207, 209-211, 213, 214, 216, 217
Evaluation	9, 11, 13, 19, 21, 23, 25, 27, 29, 31, 32, 35, 47, 49, 51, 55, 57, 59, 61, 67, 71, 77-79, 85, 87, 91, 98, 100, 103, 105, 115, 118, 121, 122, 124, 125, 129, 131, 133, 135, 137, 141, 154, 155, 159, 169, 173, 177, 179, 189, 181, 191, 197, 198, 204, 207, 208, 209, 210, 211, 216, 231-245

Unit I
Exploring Creative Design

Learning Objectives

In this unit, the students will achieve the following objectives:

Understanding Art

- Understand and define art terms used to describe the elements and principles of design
- Associate colors with moods and feelings, and different media with different effects
- Understand the techniques used to produce printing, graphics, and other common designs

Creating Art

- Create collages out of a variety of natural and man-made objects
- Practice several types of printing
- Create art out of letters and words
- Design artworks for specific purposes of communication

Appreciating Art

- Express opinions, based on context, about various designs
- Recognize and discuss the wealth of graphic artworks in their environment
- Appreciate the collages of famous artists, recognizing their unique use of materials

Unit Strands

A strand consists of a group of related lessons where the student is expected to begin with one of the lesson choices available on the far left (arranged vertically), complete it, proceed horizontally to the next group of choices, make a choice and complete the lesson, and so forth, until the entire sequence has been completed. (See page v for complete instructions on using strands.) the unit strands for this unit are diagramed below and at the top of the next column.

Strand A: The Art of Designing

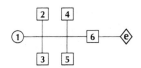

Strand B: Printmaking

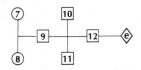

Strand C: Letters and Words

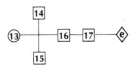

Background Information

Unit I, Exploring Creative Design, is intended to introduce the principles and elements of design to students in a straightforward manner. The unit opener discusses these basic elements and principles clearly and concisely. Students are also immediately given a piece of information that is crucial for the unit—the idea that art is all around us.

In the early lessons on collage, the students learn to see the elements of design in everyday objects. Thus, knowledge (about design elements) and correct application of that knowledge are quickly tested in a series of simple lessons requiring the use of several different techniques and media. Be certain that students do not, due to the simplicity and "fun" of these lessons, underestimate the importance of collages in the history of art, however. Remind them that these types of works by Braque and Picasso have played an important part in 20th-century art, serving as avant-garde forms of expression.

The printing lessons, lessons 7–12, require that students learn techniques that are new to them; these lessons are thus more difficult. The students will need closer supervision and instruction when attempting to master these skills. Be certain from the start that the students grasp the fact that images to be printed are in the reversed form for transferring onto the printing medium. Also use these lessons to point out again that art is all around us—on the printed page, in fabrics with prints, even in the natural world where fossils and weather elements have left their imprints.

The last five lessons deal with art as visual communication. Remind the students that signs and symbols,

1

if not words, have been used since prehistoric times for purposes of communication. Cavemen recorded events with symbols. Greeks decorated their pottery with elaborate geometrical designs and symbols. Modern men still use universal symbols to impart information. Bring the students to see the symbolism used in signs and advertisements as a form of art. Open their eyes to the art around them—in the creative impact of words, in effective layouts, and in dynamic designs. Once students can relate their artwork to the outside world, they can learn to use all the visual stimuli found there to create more complex designs.

Strategies for Motivation

Students are influenced by art objects and designs around them. They are constantly exposed to posters, logos, emblems, collages, and a host of other visual images. Throughout this unit, the students are guided to develop their powers of observation, their sense of color harmony, their feeling for design and composition. By observing, they will learn about designs and apply what they learn to improve their skills. Therefore, it is useful to relate what the students are doing in creative design with what they see around them. The following are suggestions for activities that serve this purpose. (See the individual lesson guides for specific applications.)

- Ask students to create a class scrapbook composed of magazine cutouts of logos, letter designs, etc.
- Talk about common signs being used for visual communication.
- Have an appreciation lesson on designs. Ask the students to bring in logos, emblems, trademarks, and posters and to use terms they have learned to discuss them.
- Invite local designers to give talks.

Extending Art

Exploring Art

The Exploring Art feature for Unit I extends students' art skills by directing them to create posters. It gives detailed guidelines for focus, design, color choice, and lettering. Explain the importance of considering not only the subject but also the intended audience and place of display before starting on a design. Discuss, for instance, the ways an anti-litter poster for a small kindergarten classroom might differ from a highway billboard on the same theme. Have available books showing various typefaces (obtainable from typesetting companies) so that students can see

a wide range of lettering styles. To further extend the lesson:

- Assign students to watch the local news or read the local daily paper for a week, each day noting down the two issues that are most meaningful to them. At the end of the week, students can use their notes to choose poster themes.
- Annual poster contests are sponsored by many national and local organizations (the National Safety Council and the Lung Association are two examples). Encourage students to enter their work in national, state, or local contests.

Additional Activities

Visits to see how actual printing and graphic work is done are invaluable experiences for the students. The following are two suggestions:

- Visit a printing press so the students can see the printing process.
- Visit a museum or art gallery to view how artists deal with design elements and the problem of composition. Prepare for such a field trip by previewing the works the students will see and preparing comments about them.

Evaluating Procedures

As noted in the introduction to this book, evaluation in art classes poses unique problems for the teacher. (See pages vii-viii.) The Learning Outcomes address the need for self-evaluation and test the students on the details of what they have learned. However, the teacher still needs some means of determining the extent of a student's application of specifics to a solid core of basic art knowledge. Three things are involved in this type of evaluation:

1. A written test of the student's recall of important facts.
2. An examination of the student's artwork in terms of the achievement of certain previously stated goals.
3. An oral discussion with the student involving his or her comments on a particular piece of art.

These three evaluative components for Unit I are explained below.

Vocabulary

Students who complete this unit should be able to define and correctly use the art terms listed on the following page. A written test on the unit should, then, be based on these terms.

abstract
advertising
balance
block
block printing
block relief
brayer
calligraphy
center of interest
collage
color
contrast
design
elements of design
emphasis
graphic design
line
logo
media
monogram
monoprint
movement

nib
pattern
principles of design
print
printing press
profile
proportion
rhythm
shape
silhouette
slogan
space
stained glass
texture
trademark
transparent
unified
unity
value
variety
visual
visualize

Skills

The artworks students create in this unit should meet the standards listed below. Be certain that the students are aware of these standards both as they plan and as they work. You may choose to keep the list posted throughout the time spent on this unit.
Collages:
• There is variation in the sizes, shapes, colors, and textures of objects used in the collage.
• Overlapping shapes and informal balance are used in the collage design.
Printmaking:
• Time is taken to cut the design clearly and correctly.
• The design prints right side up, revealing an understanding of the reverse nature of the printing process.
Graphics:
• Letters are legible, and shapes are clearly defined.
• Correct proportion is employed.

Application of Knowledge

Listening to a student talk about an artwork can give you a true sense of how much the student understands the basic elements and principles of design. However, the planning behind such a discussion is important. First, the work to be discussed must be chosen in advance and studied by the teacher. Questions must be written that will lead the student into

the correct areas of emphasis. Last, the discussion should be arranged to take place on a one-to-one basis so that the more reticent students are not left out of a group discussion.

A suggested artwork to use for discussion purposes in this unit is the colorful collage by Norman Laliberté entitled *The Wiesbaden Special.*

Supplementary Material and Resources

Teacher Resources

Lidstone, John. *Design Activities for the Classroom.*
    Worcester, Mass.: Davis Publications, Inc., 1977.
This is an interesting and informative book with useful illustrations of students' work. It deals with the creation of straw sculpture, wire sculpture, tempera design, cardboard printing, and the creation of slides for projection.

Lord, Lois. *Collage and Construction in School.*
    Worcester, Mass.: Davis Publications.,1970.
This is a useful book with practical suggestions and examples of collage, construction, and wire sculpture. Along with simple explanations of the various techniques are examples of students' work.

Printmaking. Milwaukee, Wis.: Sax Arts and Crafts.
    Filmstrip
This is a sixty-minute video showing how simple materials and tools can be used to create effective designs.

Rowland, Kurt. *Learning to See.* 5 volumes. New
    York: Van Nostrand Reinhold Co., 1968.
This is a very useful series of books with teachers' notes on various aspects of design. Book 1 deals with patterns seen around us. Book 2 deals with form, including practice exercises to do with simple three-dimensional blocks. Book 3 involves movement in design, and Book 4 deals with rhythm in design. Book 5 deals with visual communication and the artistic environment.

Tissue Paper Art. Milwaukee, Wis.: Sax Arts and
    Crafts. Filmstrip
This sixty-minute video shows what can be done with little bits of torn paper to create simple, fascinating collages. It illustrates the use of warm and cool colors for effect and the use of patterns in designing.

Search for Design. Modesto, Calif.: Nasco Arts Programs, 1984: Slides.
This program helps students find ideas for designs. The program stimulates thinking and creativity by helping students discover design possibilities in everyday situations.

TEACHING SUGGESTIONS for Lessons 1–17

LESSON 1

Collage from Unusual Materials

Suggested Art Materials

See the art materials list in the student book.

Planning Ahead

Choose an example of a student's collage (from your past classes or from other art teachers) that you feel is very well done within the capabilities of your students. Ask the students to examine it and suggest alternative materials. Also have them suggest titles and tell why the titles are appropriate.
Additional Materials Needed:
student collage

Helpful Teaching Hints

• Have the students suggest alternative materials and titles for the collages reproduced in the text.
• Allow the students to create their own designs freely.

Safety Precautions

Be sure the room is well-ventilated if using rubber cement, and that you store it in a safe place away from open flames.

Book Strands

Book strand 13, Artistic Surprises, and book strand 23, A Sense of Motion, include this lesson in their diagrams, pictured below. See pages xv and xvii, respectively, for a complete description of these strands.

Artistic Surprises   A Sense of Motion

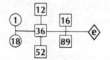   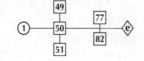

LESSON 2

Artistic Messages from Music

Suggested Art Materials

See the art materials list for this lesson in the student book.

Planning Ahead

• Ask the students to bring their favorite records or tapes for use in this lesson. (You should plan on playing several different kinds of music and having the students respond to each with a sketch. They can then each choose a favorite to complete fully.)
• Begin the lesson by describing a feeling and letting the students suggest a color that represents it.

Helpful Teaching Hints

• Spend some time talking about colors and their effects on people.
• Have the students name textures and patterns that represent a certain feeling.

Safety Precautions

Be sure the room is well-ventilated if using rubber cement, and that you store it in a safe place away from open flames.

Book Strands

Book strand 2, Abstract Puzzles, and book strand 22, Recognizing Rhythm, include this lesson in their diagrams, pictured below. See pages xiii and xvii, respectively, for a complete description of these strands.

Abstract Puzzles   Recognizing Rhythm

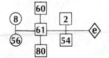   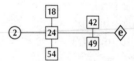

LESSON 3

The Glow of Tissue Paper

Suggested Art Materials

See the art materials list for this lesson in the student book.

Planning Ahead

Get the students thinking about texture by having them describe the textures of various types of paper: newspaper, construction paper, waxed paper, etc.

Helpful Teaching Hints

- Discuss colors with the students; have them name pairs of contrasting colors.
- Encourage the students to use many different shapes in their collages.
- Talk about developing artwork through chance. Explain that the new designs one can discover through accident are often more refreshing than those formed from preconceived ideas.

Safety Precautions

Since some waterproof inks are permanent, remind the students to be very careful or to wear paint smocks when working with inks. Also urge the students to wash any ink off the skin immediately, since inks are easily absorbed through the skin.

Book Strand

Book strand 6, Enjoying Color, includes this lesson in its diagram, pictured below. See page xiv for a complete description of this strand.

Enjoying Color

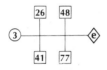

LESSON 4

Stained Glass Windows

Suggested Art Materials

See the art materials list in the student book.

Helpful Teaching Hints

Mount sheets of cellophane paper (primary colors) in cardboard frames. Display these on an overhead projector, overlapping two colors to show the secondary color created.
Additional Materials Needed:
overhead projector

Related Art Career (glass worker):

In years past, stained-glass artisans created ornate windows that still add beauty to many churches and cathedrals throughout the world. Today, the stained-glass handicraft, an occupation using skill with the hands, has experienced renewed public interest. A basic art education at a college or art school is a good foundation for this career. Knowledge of the craft, its materials and tools, can also be gained through specialty classes or practical experience.

Many glass workers market their artwork through craft or trade shows. They often join a craft organization through which their work is exhibited at local or regional mall or sidewalk shows. Some also combine their time and resources to operate cooperative centers. Because these types of business operations require financial expenditures before items are sold, glass workers will often turn to teaching their specialty at adult or community centers for extra income.

Another career for those interested in working with glass is that of the glazier, one who cuts, fits, and installs various types of glass, such as pre-assembled stained glass or mirrors in stores, office buildings, homes, or automobiles.

Gather a collection of pictures or slides that show various stained glass windows in churches, buildings, and homes. Note how the artists have combined colors and shapes into dazzling designs that reflect sunlight.

Safety Precautions

State two rules for the use of sharp instruments:
(1) Always cut away from the body.
(2) Keep fingers out of the path of cutting tools.

Book Strands

Book strand 16, being a Designer, and book strand 18, Seeing Shapes, include this lesson in their diagrams, pictured below. See page xvi for a complete description of these strands.

Being a Designer   Seeing Shapes

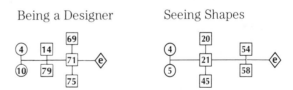

LESSON 5

Shadow Pictures

Suggested Art Materials

See the art materials list for this lesson in the student book.

Helpful Teaching Hints

Students will enjoy drawing life-sized silhouettes of one another:

(1) Tack a sheet of white paper to the wall.
(2) Have a student stand one or two feet away from the paper.
(3) Direct the light from an overhead projector toward the student.
(4) Have another student draw the outline of the shadow that is cast.
(5) Then have the student cut the silhouette out of black paper and mount it on white or other contrasting color.

Additional Materials Needed:
overhead projector

Safety Precautions

Be sure the room is well-ventilated if using rubber cement, and that you store it in a safe place away from open flames.

Book Strands

Book strand 1, Thinking with Contours, and book strand 18, Seeing Shapes, include this lesson in their diagrams, pictured below. See pages xiii and xvi, respectively, for a complete description of these strands.

Thinking with Contours   Seeing Shapes

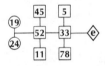 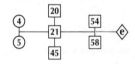

LESSON 6

Art from Nature

Suggested Art Materials

See the art materials list for this lesson in the student book.

Planning Ahead

Tell the students in advance that they should collect interesting natural objects for this lesson. You might even want to set up a daily "show and tell" period for the week preceding this lesson. Students can show their most interesting objects and describe the details that attracted them (special colors or textures, for example).

Helpful Teaching Hints

Display pictures of animals and plants for the students to look at in case they cannot decide what types of images their collages will portray.

Safety Precautions

Be sure the room is well-ventilated if using strong glue, and that you store it in a safe place away from open flames.

Book Strands

Book strand 9, Composing Pictures and Designs, and book strand 19, Form in Art, include this lesson in the diagrams, pictured below. See pages xv and xvi, respectively, for a complete description of these strands.

Composing Pictures   Form in Art
and Designs

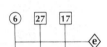 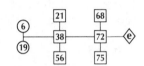

LESSON 7

Printing with Natural Objects

Suggested Art Materials

See the art materials list for this lesson in the student book.

Planning Ahead

Have a collection of leaves available for the students to use when printing. Discuss with them which leaves are best for this purpose (those with clear veins in relief).

Additional Materials Needed:
leaves

Helpful Teaching Hints

If the students have collected flat objects to use, or if they are using leaves, encourage them to overlap the objects for a more interesting design.

Book Strand

Book strand 7, Exploring Textures, includes this lesson in its diagram, pictured below. See page xiv for a complete description of this strand.

Exploring Textures

LESSON 8

Printing with Man-Made Objects

Suggested Art Materials

See the art materials list for this lesson in the student book.

Helpful Teaching Hints

Take some time to discuss the textural qualities of the objects the students will use. Ask them to describe the patterns the various objects will make. Then give the students plenty of time to experiment before they attempt making organized designs.

Safety Precautions

Remind the students to be careful not to get ink on their clothing and to wash ink off skin immediately.

Book Strand

Book strand 2, Abstract Puzzles, includes this lesson in its diagram, pictured below. See page xiii for a complete description of this strand.

Abstract Puzzles

LESSON 9

One-Time Printmaking

Suggested Art Materials

See the art materials list for this lesson in the student book.

Helpful Teaching Hints

- Spread a layer of ink on a piece of glass. Make different marks on it to show density, texture, and pattern. See if the students can describe what the design will be like when printed.
- Allow plenty of time for the students to experiment before they create their prints.

Safety Precautions

Remind the students to be careful not to get ink on their clothing and to wash ink off skin immediately.

Book Strand

Book strand 11, Imagineering, includes this lesson in its diagram, pictured below. See page xv for a complete description of this strand.

Imagineering

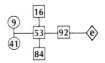

LESSON 10

Relief Prints and Patterns

Suggested Art Materials

See the art materials list for this lesson in the student book.

Planning Ahead

Collect nature photographs (from *Audubon*, Sierra Club publications, calendars, etc.) for the students to thumb through for design possibilities.
Additional Materials Needed:
nature photographs

Helpful Teaching Hints

- Make sure the students are careful when gluing. If the string is not adhered properly, the whole process will be ruined.
- Students may prefer to use tempera paint rather than ink, since the range of colors is broader.

Book Strand

Book strand 16, Being a Designer, includes this lesson in its diagram, pictured below. see page xvi for a complete description of this strand.

Being a Designer

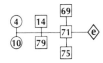

LESSON 11

Printing with Vegetables

Suggested Art Materials

See the art materials list for this lesson in the student book.

Planning Ahead

You will need to provide the root vegetables for this lesson. Bring enough so that students will have some extras to experiment with.

Helpful Teaching Hints

Make sure the students understand that the parts they carve out will *not* show in their prints.

Safety Precautions

Remind the students to have dry hands when using carving tools. Also remind them to cut *away* from their bodies and to keep their fingers out of the path of the sharp tools.

Book Strand

Book strand 1, Thinking with Contours, includes this lesson in its diagram, pictured below. See page xiii for a complete description of this strand.

Thinking with Contours

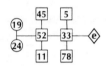

LESSON 12

Printed Lettering

Suggested Art Materials

See the art materials list for this lesson in the student book.

Helpful Teaching Hints

- Have students make a list of adjectives that reflect their own personalities, and then think of visual translations for each word. For example, the word *happy* may look like bubbles or lines curving upward or a smiling face.
- After students have created the design on thin paper, have them turn it over and hold it up to a light source. When looking at the design backwards, they can readily observe changes they might want to make to achieve a more balanced design before transferring it to the linoleum block.
- When pressing the inked block onto a sheet of paper, a smoother, complete print will result if the student firmly rolls the back of the linoleum block with a clean, dry brayer.
- When printing the design, corners of the block will leave some markings even though the linoleum has

been cut away. Students may want to create a border design on the edges of the block as an alternative.
- If students are working with more than one ink color, have a separate smooth surface and brayer for each color. Make sure students clean the linoleum blocks thoroughly (in the crevices and on the outer edges of each block) before applying a different colored ink. The printed results will be clean, pure colors and the inks will not appear muddied.

Safety Precautions

(1) Caution the students to have dry hands when using the cutting tools and to cut *away* from their bodies, keeping fingers out of the path.

(2) Remind the students to keep the ink off their clothing and to wash any ink off their skin immediately.

Book Strand

Book strand 13, Artistic Surprises, includes this lesson in its diagram, pictured below. See page xv for a complete description of this strand.

Artistic Surprises

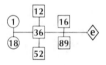

LESSON 13

Calligraphy and Fine Handwriting

Suggested Art Materials

See the art materials list for this lesson in the student book.

Planning Ahead

Shave a piece of chalk to resemble the pen nib of a calligraphy pen. Use this piece of chalk to write words using letters of different sizes. Ask the students to pick out the words that look the best. Then lead them into a discussion of proportion in letters. *Additional Materials Needed:*
chalk, chalkboard

Helpful Teaching Hints

- Relate proportion in letters to the widths of pens in calligraphy.

- It takes some time to get used to calligraphy tools. You may choose to let students spend a whole period practicing and then another period producing the artwork.
- Have literature anthologies, poetry collections, and quote collections available for your students to use to find excerpts. Also encourage them to write original sayings and poems to use.*

Additional Materials Needed:
*literary resources

Safety Precautions

Remind the students that waterproof ink can stain permanently and to wash it off immediately if it gets on the skin or clothing.

Book Strand

Book strand 8, Studying Lines, includes this lesson in its diagram, pictured below. See page xiv for a complete description of this strand.

Studying Lines

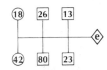

LESSON 14

Letter Design

Suggested Art Materials

See the art materials list for this lesson in the student book.

Planning Ahead

Collect examples of lettering in advertising that catch your eye.
Additional Materials Needed:
advertisements that use letters

Helpful Teaching Hints

- Discuss the examples you have brought in:
  (1) How is the style appropriate to the content?
  (2) What other products could have advertisements using this style of letters?
- Ask the students to think about their personalities and create name plates using a style of letter that denotes their strongest character traits. Remind them to use correctly proportioned letters.

Related Art Careers (commercial artist)

Commercial artist, or designer, is a broad job title encompassing several specific careers in the field of applied arts, or art put to practical use. Detailed information on some of these can be found in the following lessons: graphic designer, Lesson 15; illustrator, Lesson 23; and industrial designer, Lesson 59. Ask students to think of other job titles that might be included in the field of commercial art.

Book Strands

Book strand 16, Being a Designer, and book strand 20, Sizing Up Relationships, include this lesson in their diagrams, pictured below. See page xvi for a complete description of these strands.

Being a Designer   Sizing Up Relationships

   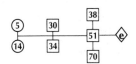

LESSON 15

Monograms and Trademarks

Suggested Art Materials

See the art materials list for this lesson in the student book.

Planning Ahead

Collect examples of company logos and trademarks. Discuss with the class how each is applicable to the type of business.
Additional Materials Needed:
company logos and trademarks

Helpful Teaching Hints

Talk with the students about their personal hobbies, interests, likes, and dislikes. Discuss how an appropriate motif can relate to the subject matter, and have the students suggest motifs for other students' interests. (Example: A student interested in football could make a monogram in the shape of a football.)

Safety Precautions

Remind the students that waterproof ink can stain permanently and to wash it off immediately if it gets on the skin or clothing.

Related Art Careers (graphic designer)

The job titles graphic designer and graphic artists are generally used interchangeably, although graphic artists often work in the field of printmaking only. The graphic designer, one who creates and executes plans for a project, is the planner of the printed page. The designer organizes the type, lettering, and visuals in a layout and selects ink, paper, and printing processes to be used to create the total image. The projects can range from books, magazines, packages, posters, signs, and advertisements to the newer multi-media fields of computer graphics, film strips, slides, and tapes. A good art and design program will prepare the designer to work with a variety of media and materials, including photography, typeface, manuscripts, silk screen, and lettering.

Have available advertising brochures, magazines, books, or other materials that have been done by graphic designers. Discuss specific aspects of the design, such as layout, clarity of information, typeface, and visuals.

Book Strand

Book strand 9, Composing Pictures and Designs, includes this lesson in its diagram, pictured below. See page xv for a complete description of this strand.

Composing Pictures and Designs

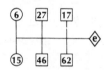

LESSON 16

Word Pictures

Suggested Art Materials

See the art materials list for this lesson in the student book.

Helpful Teaching Hints

Plan this lesson as an extension of the previous two lessons. Students should, by now, be relating visual imagery to meaning, and the illustrations in the text should enable them to apply information gained in previous lessons to this lesson.

Book Strands

Book strand 11, Imagineering, and book strand 13, Artistic Surprises, include this lesson in their dia-grams, pictured below. See page xv for complete descriptions of these strands.

Imagineering 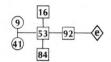 Artistic Surprises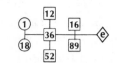

LESSON 17

Art for Advertising

Suggested Art Materials

See the art materials list for this lesson in the student book.

Planning Ahead

Collect old magazines with plenty of pictures. Students can cut these up for visual images to include on their posters.
Additional Materials Needed:
magazines

Helpful Teaching Hints

- Explain that graphic designs are normally flat and two-dimensional. Refer the students to well-known billboards, food packages, and other advertisements that use graphic designs.
- Introduce photomontage to the students. Discuss the pros and cons of this technique as compared to the simplicity of other techniques. Ask them to decide which type of design would be best for a poster. (Stress that it depends on the poster's purpose.)

Book Strand

Book strand 9, Composing Pictures and Designs, includes this lesson in its diagram, pictured below. See page xv for a complete description of this strand.

Composing Pictures and Designs

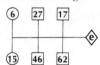

Exploring Art

Designing a Poster

See page 2 for an explanation and teaching suggestions.

Unit II
Drawing Objects and Figures

Learning Objectives

In this unit, students will achieve the following objectives:

Understanding Art

- Explain and define art terms, media, and techniques used for drawing
- Understand, through observation and experimentation, that light, texture, space, and dimensions affect artistic conception of objects
- Understand the concepts of depth, horizon, proportion, symmetry, and perspective

Creating Art

- Draw a variety of flat and curvilinear objects using line, shading, and texture
- Demonstrate ability to draw objects in perspective
- Experiment with a variety of art materials
- Draw human and animal forms in correct proportions
- Explore, through imitation, the drawing styles of well-known artists

Appreciating Art

- Study the works of great artists for concept, style, and aesthetic qualities
- Appreciate the expression of mood and emotion through artworks
- Understand and express ideas about the aesthetic qualities of others' artworks as well as one's own

Unit Strands

A strand consists of a group of related lessons where the student is expected to begin with one of the lesson choices available on the far left (arranged vertically), complete it, proceed horizontally to the next group of choices, make a choice and complete the lesson, and so forth, until the entire sequence has been completed. (See page v for complete instructions on using strands.) The unit strands for this unit are diagrammed at the top of the next column.

Strand D: Lines, Shapes, and Textures

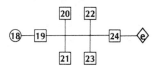

Strand E: Drawing Methods and Media

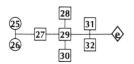

Strand F: Faces and Figures

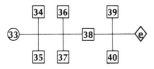

Background Information

Unit II, Drawing Objects and Figures, is designed to introduce the techniques of drawing, from the simple to the complex. As students progress, they will learn to observe accurately and then translate their visual experiences to paper, using a variety of art materials and tools with increasing confidence.

Introductory lessons 18–22 guide the students through basic drawing techniques and concepts. They teach the students to observe accurately and to develop visual, mental, and manual connections that are essential to learning to draw. When the students complete these lessons, they will be able to draw the contours or outlines of objects, make shading gradations from light to dark of planes and round objects, reproduce the different textural qualities of objects, and produce a composition (drawn with a variety of materials) that demonstrates learned skills.

Lessons 23 and 24 can also be considered important basal lessons, as they concentrate on an important skill: observation. By comparing similarities in scientific and artistic observational methods, these lessons increase students' abilities to observe. Lessons 31 and 32 also emphasize the importance of observation by introducing the concept of visual memory.

Perhaps the most unifying component of this unit, however, is the reproduction of drawings. The introduction of drawings by well-known artists—Audubon, Picasso, Monet, Dürer, Rembrandt, and others—from the start of this unit provides stimulating examples of insightful observation and individualistic rendering. By showing that similar subjects—a chair, an animal, the human figure—are observed and drawn well in a different style by each artist, lessons that use reproductions of art help to develop students' confidence in their own emerging skills. Through imitating a variety of styles of great artists, students extend their drawing skills and become involved mentally and emotionally in how those artists viewed life around them.

Throughout the remaining lessons of the unit, relevant examples from art history and the teaching of aesthetic awareness are interwoven with skill development experiences. Lessons 39 and 40, for example, serve as natural discussion openers for the topics of art history and aesthetic judgment. Comparisons should be made among artists' styles, showing the differences in their use of line, their techniques for rendering light and dark, their approaches to composition, and their concepts of subject matter.

Examples of straight drawing lessons are lessons 33–38, designed to teach competency in figure drawing, from simple profiles to the figure in action. Students learn to draw the human head and figure in correct proportion, using line and shading techniques learned in previous lessons. They also learn how to enlarge a picture or photo by using the grid system and how to depict facial expressions and the body in action.

Supplement these figure drawing lessons with increased exposure to well-known artists' drawings. Selections from the sketchbooks and notebooks of Leonardo, Michelangelo, Picasso, and other artists should be used. Quick sketches which are multiple views of the same object are particularly useful to the novice. Though the text illustrations have been chosen to depict a particular style or concept approach, they may also serve as a basis for teaching students about how styles of drawing the human figure have changed over the centuries, and how these styles have been aesthetically appreciated or viewed. The use of the book's examples should be balanced with the use of current popular examples of artworks showing the human figure—record album covers, cartoons, or advertisements. Such examples provide students with a sense of the immediate relevancy of their work, as well as a sense of continuity with a long history of art.

Lessons 27 and 30 are designed to develop students' abilities to conceptualize the unity of a composition in space and then render it using correct perspective. These lessons encourage students to develop their perceptual abilities from different eye levels, create the effect of space between three-dimensional objects, and create the illusions of nearness and distance through delineation and shading techniques. Again, these lessons can be supplemented with discussions about the history and changing aesthetics of the use of perspective in art. Display examples of pre-Medieval, Medieval, and Renaissance ways of depicting space and distance, both interior and exterior, so that the students can understand the evolution of this important artistic concept.

Strategies for Motivation

Unit II provides a foundation for developing skills in other art forms—painting, collage, printmaking, sculpture, ceramics, and fabric arts. For example, the students' perceptual abilities are sharpened while they are encouraged to develop the dexterity needed for drawing. The following suggestions will increase students' perception of objects (see individual lesson guides for specific applications):

- Contour drawing—outline objects to be drawn with colored yarn or twine.
- Use portable flood lamps to dramatize effects of light and dark planes.
- Have the students, with their eyes closed, feel different objects with distinctive textures in order to visualize tactile perceptions.

It is important to bring the outside world inside to increase the students' interest in the lessons and to emphasize the idea that art can stem from the everyday world. Use these activities to achieve these goals:

- When setting up still life compositions to be drawn, utilize car and motorcycle parts in some of them.
- Have the students bring in their favorite comic strips or children's books which illustrate the current art lesson.
- Use photographs of the local community for lessons on perspective.

Extending Art

Exploring Art

The Exploring Art feature at the end of Unit II extends art skills beyond the classroom by guiding students in starting sketchbooks. It gives suggestions for subjects to sketch and for sketching tools to use. Emphasize that one advantage of a sketchbook is that it is portable; encourage students to find subjects in their home or leisure environments. Explain the value of spontaneity in sketching. Specific extensions of this Exploring Art feature could include the following:

- Suggest that students try making two sketches of the same subject, using two different sketching tools; for example, a student could use crayon to sketch a leaf, then use pencil to sketch the same leaf, and compare the effects each tool achieves.
- Assign a series of sketches of the same subject, to be brought to class and used as the basis for a finished piece of art.

Additional Activities

A number of lessons in this unit may be extended in ways that enhance their creative and teaching potential and provide additional motivation stimuli to the students. Below are some general suggestions, but you should also see the individual lesson guides for specific applications.

- Bring a number of small animals for the class to sketch, or visit a zoo for the same purpose, placing the emphases on line, texture, and movement.
- Invite a local athlete to pose for action sketches of the human figure.
- Encourage the students to carry and use sketchbooks outside of class.
- Have the students set up an exhibit of their own work, with a reception for guests.
- Use local artists, craftspersons, or printers to demonstrate their crafts and act as career resource people.
- Visit appropriately related exhibits of artworks at local galleries and museums.

Evaluating Procedures

As noted in the introduction to this book, evaluation in art classes poses unique problems for the teacher. (See pages vii–viii.) The Learning Outcomes address the need for self-evaluation and test the students on the details of what they have learned. However, the teacher still needs some means of determining the student's application of specifics to a solid core of basic art knowledge. Three things are involved in this type of evaluation:

1. A written test of the student's recall of important facts
2. An examination of the student's artwork in terms of the achievement of certain previously stated goals

3. An oral discussion with the student involving his or her comments on a particular piece of art

These three evaluative components for Unit II are explained below.

Vocabularly

Students who complete this unit should be able to define and correctly use the art terms listed below. A written test on the unit should, then, be based on these terms.

blind contour drawing	proportion
compass	protractor
contour	Renaissance
cylinder	scale
dimension	scale drawing
freehand	set square
genius	shading
gradation	space
grid	sphere
horizon	style
landscape	symmetrical
media	template
modified contour drawing	texture
	three-dimensional
mount	T-square
mural	unity
perspective	value
plane	visualize
portrait	visual memory
profile	

Skills

The artworks students create in this unit should meet the standards listed below. Be certain that the students are aware of these standards both as they plan and as they work. You may choose to keep the list posted throughout the time spent on this unit.

- Lines are varied from thin to thick, and gradation is used.
- The negative space, the space between objects, is an important part of the composition.
- Perspective is shown through overlapping and through making foreground objects bigger and more detailed.
- Correct body proportions are used.
- The drawing reveals what is actually seen rather than depicting a stereotyped image.

Application of Knowledge

Listening to a student talk about an artwork can give you a true sense of how much the student understands the basic elements and principles of design.

However, the planning behind such a discussion is important. First, the work to be disucssed must be chosen in advance and studied by the teacher. Questions must be written that will lead the student into the correct areas of emphasis. Last, the discussion should be arranged to take place on a one-to-one basis so that the more reticent students are not left out of a group discussion.

Suggested artworks to use for discussion purposes in this unit are any of the pencil sketches of cities done by Eric Nivelle and the painting by Paul Sample entitled *Boys' Ski Outing.*

Supplementary Materials and Resources

Teacher Resources

Edwards, Betty. *Drawing on the Right Side of the Brain.* Los Angeles: J.P. Tarcher, Inc., 1979.
A course in enhancing creativity and confidence, this book uses self-instruction methods.

Mendelowitz, Daniel M. *Drawing* and *A Study Guide.* New York: Holt, Rinehart, and Winston, Inc., 1967.
Drawing discusses the history of drawing, from cave drawings to 20th-century Expressionism. Covered are line, form, value, texture, media, and imagination. Numerous reproductions are included. The supplementary study guide provides a variety of specific activities suitable for classroom use.

Nicolaides, Kimon. *The Natural Way to Draw.* Boston: Houghton Mifflin Co., 1969.
This book covers contour, gesture, modeling of human figure drawing (some animals), memory drawing, quick sketches, and drawing in ink. It is illustrated with reproductions of the works of master draftsmen—Rodin, Michelangelo, Rembrandt, etc.

Richter, Jean Paul, ed. *The Notebooks of Leonardo da Vinci,* 2 vols. New York: Dover Publications, Inc., 1970.
Compiled from the original manuscripts, the *Notebooks* contain numerous drawings, including pictures of Leonardo's inventions, and his notes and thoughts, showing his genius.

Simon, Howard. *Techniques of Drawing.* New York: Dover Publications, Inc., 1963.
This book gives examples and problems to solve concerning line, form, movement, structure of the human body, composition, use of perspective, outdoor sketching, and drawing animals. Technique and use of media are covered. Many examples by the author and well-known artists are included.

Toney, Anthony. *Creative Painting and Drawing.* New York: Dover Publications, Inc., 1966.
Discussions, as applied to painting and drawing, about ways of seeing, the creative process, symbolism, distortion, line, shape, space, value, color, texture, organization, and materials are included in this source. Useful black-and-white quick figure sketches by the author are also featured.

Zappalorti, Robert. *Drawing Sharp Focus Still Lifes.* New York: Watson-Guptill Publications, 1981.
This book shows how to draw objects composed of all types of materials. It also includes discussions on perspective, proportion, rendering, and use of materials. The book is illustrated by the author.

Student Resources

Raboff, Ernest. *Leonardo da Vinci.* Garden City, New York: Doubleday and Co., 1978.
This is a volume in a series which includes books about Klee, Chagall, Picasso, Renoir, Van Gogh, Rousseau, Toulouse-Lautrec, Dürer, Rembrandt, Gauguin, Velásquez, Michelangelo, Raphael, and Frederic Remington. Each volume is an excellent, vibrant way of introducing art history to youngsters.

TEACHING SUGGESTIONS for Lessons 18-40

LESSON 18

Doodles That Come Alive

Suggested Art Materials

See the art materials list for this lesson in the student book.

Helpful Teaching Hints

Have the students look at any doodles they might have made in their notebooks for other classes. With the students' permission, pass some of these doodles around, pointing out that many of them are pictures, even though they probably started out as mere lines. Explain that this ability to turn mere shapes and lines into a picture is actually a form of artistic vision. Thus, no student should feel like he or she has no artistic talent, since even doodling reveals some inherent artistry.

Book Strands

Book strand 8, Studying Lines, and book strand 13, Artistic Surprises, include this lesson in their diagrams, pictured below. See pages xiv and xv, respectively, for complete descriptions of these strands.

Studying Lines

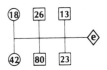

Artistic Surprises

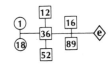

LESSON 19

Contour Drawing

Suggested Art Materials

See the art materials list for this lesson in the student book.

Planning Ahead

Introduce the concept of contours by outlining the contours of solid objects with colored string or tape. Ask the students to focus on this string, running their eyes along the lines it forms. This will enable them to later find contours on their own, without clues, as the lesson requires.
Additional Materials Needed:
colored string or tape

Helpful Teaching Hints

• Stress the need for concentration. Students must establish a true visual-manual connection for this lesson, so insist on no distractions.
• Have students practice outlining objects with a flashlight in a darkened room to heighten their sensitivity to the concept of contours.*
• Use drawings by Matisse and Picasso as examples of contour drawing.**
Additional Materials Needed:
 *flashlight
**drawings by Matisse and Picasso

Book Strand

Book Strand 1, Thinking with Contours, includes this lesson in its diagram, pictured at the top of the next column. See page xiii for a description of this strand.

Thinking with Contours

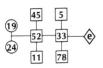

LESSON 20

Light on Flat Objects

Suggested Art Materials

See the art materials list for this lesson in the student book.

Helpful Teaching Hints

• Show how to effectively use a pencil to create different shades of gray. Then have the students fill a paper with such shading, using the drawings in the text for examples.
• Use floodlights to emphasize the light and dark areas of the flat objects the students are instructed to draw in this lesson.*
Additional Materials Needed:
*floodlights

Book Strand

Book Strand 4, Art with Flat Planes, includes this lesson in its diagram, pictured below. See page xiv for a complete description of this strand.

Art with Flat Planes

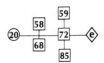

LESSON 21

Light on Rounded Objects

Suggested Art Materials

See the art materials list for this lesson in the student book.

Helpful Teaching Hints

• Define *gradation* as meaning a slow change from light to dark. Show how to use the side of a pencil to achieve smoother gradation of shading, and how to use an eraser to lighten areas.
• Before the students begin their drawings, have them paste strips of gray paper of different values on round objects to dramatize the effect of shading.

They can refer to these when drawing.*

Additional Materials Needed:
* round objects, strips of gray paper of varying values, paste

Book Strand

Book strand 14, From Observation to Imagination, includes this lesson in its diagram, pictured below. See page xv for a complete description of this strand.

From Observation to Imagination

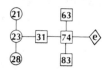

LESSON 22

Discovering and Drawing Textures

Suggested Art Materials

See the art materials list for this lesson in the student book.

Planning Ahead

Prepare, possibly on a handout, the following introductions to terms that students should comprehend before tackling this lesson.
* *Design*—a mixture of arranging and inventing
* *Texture*—the look and/or feeling of a surface (rough, smooth, silky, etc.)
* *Contrast*—a big difference between two things

Helpful Teaching Hints

* Have students handle, with their eyes closed, the different objects they will be drawing in this lesson. Ask them to visualize each object and then orally describe what they feel.
* Bring a small animal to class (a bird, a gerbil, a rabbit), and have the students draw it. They should concentrate on the contour, shading, and texture of the animal.*

Additional Materials Needed:
* a small animal

Book Strand

Book strand 7, Exploring Textures, includes this lesson in its diagram, pictured at the top of the next column. See page xiv for a complete description of this strand.

Exploring Textures

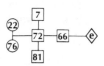

LESSON 23

Artists and Scientists as Observers

Suggested Art Materials

See the art materials list for this lesson in the student book.

Planning Ahead

* Tell the students in advance that they should bring natural objects to class to draw.
* Gather examples of botanical, medical, and biological drawings to display. Introduce the lesson by discussing how these examples demonstrate that artistic and scientific skills can be combined.

Helpful Teaching Hints

* Emphasize the importance of keen observation by showing close-ups and enlargements of things in nature. Point out that many details make up even the simplest objects, although you must look hard to see them.*
* Show artworks by Leonardo da Vinci and Audubon, discussing with the students how these men had a keen sense of scientific observation.

Additional Materials Needed:
* close-ups or enlargements of things in nature

Related Art Careers (illustrator)

The job of illustrator is usually defined more specifically by the area being illustrated. Many illustrators, for example, specialize in a certain field, such as sports, fashions, comics, technical or scientific illustration. Others prefer to practice their art for a variety of purposes and may submit their work for books and magazines, as well as other kinds of printed materials. Illustrators often attend art school or college, working in a variety of media. Knowledge of printmaking, photography, and the mechanics of printing are also important. Technical courses in mechanical drafting are needed for some illustrators. Although a college degree is helpful, the quality and style of work in a strong portfolio is equally important. Successful illustrators become observers, readers, and researchers of the subject matter they are illustrating.

John Audubon, founder of the Audubon Society, is one of the best-known scientific illustrators today. Ask students to identify and discuss other illustrators they might know about. Have them select their favorite illustrator of children's books or their favorite illustration.

Book Strands

Book strand 8, Studying Lines, and book strand 14, From Observation to Imagination, include this lesson in their diagrams, pictured below. See pages xiv and xv, respectively, for descriptions of these strands.

Studying Lines

From Observation to Imagination

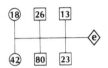 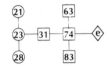

LESSON 24

Drawing Shapes and Spaces

Suggested Art Materials

See the art materials list in the student book.

Helpful Teaching Hints

Talk about how stark a picture would appear if the background spaces were totally white. Examples of landscape paintings and drawings will most effectively illustrate this. (Point out how the skies in these pictures are filled with color and details.)
Additional Materials Needed:
landscape paintings and drawings

Safety Precautions

Remind the students that waterproof ink can stain permanently and if it gets on the skin, to wash it immediately.

Book Strand

Book strand 1, Thinking with Contours, includes this lesson in its diagram, pictured below. See page xiii for a complete description of this strand.

Thinking with Contours

LESSON 25

Drawing without a Pencil

Suggested Art Materials

See the art materials list for this lesson in the student book.

Planning Ahead

Gather a variety of objects of different textures and colors that students can use for their drawings.

Helpful Teaching Hints

- Monitor the students as they practice with different drawing materials. Suggest techniques to achieve the look of texture.
- Emphasize that the use of color can create contrast. Help students experiment with color when creating depictions of texture and contrast.

Book Strand

Book strand 17, The Quest for Self-Expression, includes this lesson in its diagram, pictured below. See page xvi for a complete description of this strand.

The Quest for Self-Expression

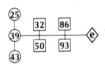

LESSON 26

Drawing with Color

Suggested Art Materials

See the art materials list for this lesson in the student book.

Helpful Teaching Hints

- Show a series of brightly colored pictures and photographs, discussing with the students whether or not each one could easily be depicted using oil pastels.*
- Point out that the boldest effects can be achieved when pastels are applied in blocks of solid colors.
- Suggest that the colors which are repeated to achieve unity be slightly differentiated in value or intensity so that monotony is avoided.
Additional Materials Needed:
* brightly colored pictures and photographs

Safety Precautions

Use turpentine only in a well-ventilated area. Keep the container labeled, capped, and in a cool place when not in use. If turpentine gets on the skin, wash immediately.

Book Strands

Book strand 6, Enjoying Color, and book strand 8, Studying Lines, include this lesson in their diagrams, pictured below. See page xiv for complete descriptions of these strands.

Enjoying Color   Studying Lines

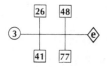 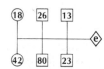

LESSON 27

Joining Up Picture Ideas

Suggested Art Materials

See the art materials list for this lesson in the student book.

Helpful Teaching Hints

This lesson is best used as an introduction to the three lessons that follow it. Unit composition is an important concept, but it should not be taught in isolation from the concept of perspective.

Safety Precautions

Be sure the room is well-ventilated if using strong glue, and that you store it in a safe place away from open flames.

Book Strand

Book strand 9, Composing Pictures and Designs, includes this lesson in its diagram, pictured below. See page xv for a complete description of this strand.

Composing Pictures and Designs

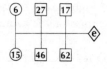

LESSON 28

Above and Below the Horizon

Suggested Art Materials

See the art materials list for this lesson in the student book.

Planning Ahead

You may wish to plan this as an outdoor lesson, first introducing the concept of horizon inside the classroom and then letting the students draw in terms of horizon outdoors, where the visual field is larger.

Helpful Teaching Hints

Explain that *horizon* means the same as *eye level*. Students are often better able to understand a concept when it is stated in terms they are already familiar with.

Book Strand

Book strand 14, from Observation to Imagination, includes this lesson in its diagram, pictured below. See page xv for a complete description of this strand.

From Observation to Imagination

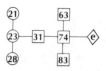

LESSON 29

Two Ways of Showing Distance

Suggested Art Materials

See the art materials list for this lesson in the student book.

Planning Ahead

Collect interior design or architectural magazines which advertise furniture. Students may choose to draw the furniture depicted in these magazines for this lesson.
Additional Materials Needed:
magazines picturing furniture

Helpful Teaching Hints

Other visual phenomena differentiating close objects from far objects are: the details in close objects can be observed; close objects are lighter in color than far objects. Advanced students may wish to use all of these elements when creating their drawings of furniture.

Safety Precautions

Be sure the room is well-ventilated if using strong glue, and that you store it in a safe place away from open flames.

Book Strand

Book strand 12, The Look of Distance, includes this lesson in its diagram, pictured below. See page xv for a complete description of this strand.

The Look of Distance

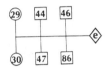

LESSON 30

Near, Far, and In Between

Suggested Art Materials

See the art materials list for this lesson in the student book.

Planning Ahead

Since this lesson addresses all aspects of perspective and composition, it is best to plan to go outside to demonstrate these concepts. The confines of a classroom and the lack of distance that can be perceived makes it harder to point out examples of the elements involved in perspective. If weather or other circumstances prohibit your going outside, have several photographs (possibly out of travel magazines or *National Geographic*) on hand to use in pointing out specific examples.

Helpful Teaching Hints

- Stress the concept that is taught only in this lesson: the effect distance has on colors.

- Give the students plenty of time (probably more than one class period) to complete their landscape drawings, since this lesson asks students to apply many concepts at once.

Book Strands

Book strand 12, The Look of Distance, and book strand 20, Sizing Up Relationships, include this lesson in their diagrams, pictured at the top of the

next column. See pages xv and xvi, respectively, for a complete description of these strands.

The Look of Distance   Sizing Up Relationships

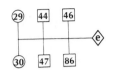   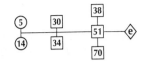

LESSON 31

Using Your Visual Memory

Suggested Art Materials

See the art materials list for this lesson in the student book.

Helpful Teaching Hints

- Stress that visual memory relies on close observations at the time of exposure to a scene.
- Students might enjoy recalling scenes from movies they have seen. Point out that the details of these scenes may be more easily recalled than those of everyday scenes, since moviegoers are specifically concentrating on what they are seeing.

Book Strand

Book strand 14, From Observation to Imagination, includes this lesson in its diagram, pictured below. See page xv for a complete description of this strand.

From Observation to Imagination

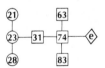

LESSON 32

Inside an Artist's World

Suggested Art Materials

See the art materials list for this lesson in the student book.

Helpful Teaching Hints

Begin the lesson by brainstorming with your students. Choosing a place everyone in the classroom is familiar with (perhaps the school gym or cafeteria), ask the students to close their eyes and visualize the details of the scene there. List these on the chalkboard, and then go with your class to the place described to see how well they remembered it.

Related Art Career (fine artist)

Vincent van Gogh pursued his desire to be an artist and nearly starved because his talent was not recognized during his lifetime. Many others who have chosen fine art painting as their career have had a similar experience. Usually, fine artists can't count on earning a living from the sale of their work alone. Many turn to teaching their art or to other related applied arts jobs as secondary sources of income.

Attending a good art school is a beginning for those who wish to pursue a career in fine arts. However, artists must usually practice their craft for many years before they are able to develop a personal art style that will enhance their work and win them recognition in this highly competitive field. Most fine artists begin by displaying their work in local or regional art shows, exhibitions, or galleries on commission.

If there are galleries or art museums in your community, consider taking your students to visit one of them. Learn about a local artist, study his or her style of art, and if possible, invite the artist to give a talk to the class about his or her career.

Book Strand

Book strand 17, The Quest for Self-Expression, includes this lesson in its diagram, pictured below. See page xvi for a complete description of this strand.

The Quest for Self-Expression

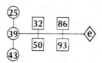

LESSON 33

Drawing Profiles

Suggested Art Materials

See the art materials list in the student book.

Helpful Teaching Hints

Use a model to clarify the proportions of the head. You may choose to use either an actual bust or sculpted head, or a student in your class. Use a measuring tape to show the actual distances between the points described in the student text.

Additional Materials Needed:
bust or sculpted head (optional), measuring tape

Book Strand

Book strand 1, Thinking with Contours, includes this lesson in its diagram, pictured below. See page xiii for a complete description of this strand.

Thinking with Contours

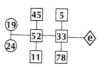

LESSON 34

Create a Face

Suggested Art Materials

See the art materials list in the student book.

Planning Ahead

Collect plenty of magazines and newspapers for the students to thumb through to find faces. Good sources might be the year-end issues of *Life*, *People*, *Rolling Stone* and *Sports Illustrated*.

Helpful Teaching Hints

- Have students look at faces in the magazines and newspapers. They will want to notice different facial features, expressions, and unique characteristics.
- Mention to students that half of any person's face is usually different from the other half; one eyebrow may be higher or thicker than the other, one nostril larger or smaller, and so on. Have them look for these details in the photographs, in a mirror, and in faces around them.
- When students are sketching the eyes, nose, mouth, and ears, point out that these features are achieved best by using mere suggestions of lines and shapes and by shading.
- Suggest to the students that they seat their selected model near a strong light source to help increase the contrast of light and dark areas on the facial features.
- Stress that sketching the head shape and facial features very lightly in the beginning will make it easier to make adjustments and reduce the amount of erasing.

- Urge the students to use their line and shading skills to make the details of their pictures realistic.

Book Strand

Book strand 15, All About People, includes this lesson in its diagram, pictured below. See page xvi for a complete description of this strand.

All About People

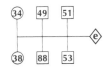

LESSON 35

Face Messages

Suggested Art Materials

See the art materials list for this lesson in the student book.

Helpful Teaching Hints

- The emphasis of this lesson is the expressiveness involved in drawing. Therefore, it is useful to start the lesson by having the students practice drawing faces that express different emotions. They can use the examples in the text as guides.
- Next, let students practice, in small groups, making faces that reflect different emotions. Closely observing others' faces in real life will help students notice how the face moves.
- Finally, give the students plenty of time to observe their own faces and decide on the expressions they wish to capture in their drawings. Have the students guess what expression each person was portraying and tell how they knew.
- Stress that getting expression into the drawing is more important than making it look like a photograph.

Book Strand

Book strand 5, Faces and Feelings, includes this lesson in its diagram, pictured below. See page xiv for a complete description of this strand.

Faces and Feelings

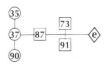

LESSON 36

Drawing Close-ups

Suggested Art Materials

See the art materials list for this lesson in the student book.

Helpful Teaching Hints

- Hold a cardboard frame in front of a student's face so that only part of the features show. Discuss how a close-up operates in this same way with the intention of emphasizing certain parts of a person or object for special effects.*
- Show how to use color to heighten the effect of a close-up.

Additional Materials Needed:
* cardboard frame

Book Strand

Book strand 13, Artistic Surprises, includes this lesson in its diagram, pictured below. See page xv for a complete description of this strand.

Artistic Surprises

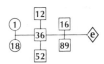

LESSON 37

Small into Large

Suggested Art Materials

See the art materials list for this lesson in the student book.

Planning Ahead

Plan on using this lesson to actually create a classroom mural showing a school or local scene of interest to the students. Have a large piece of butcher paper, paints, and measuring and drawing materials ready to use.

Helpful Teaching Hints

Refer to the works of great muralists such as Rivera and Siqueiros to point out the need for scale. Have students turn to page 217 to study the mural by Diego Rivera.

Book Strand

Book strand 5, Faces and Feelings, includes this lesson in its diagram, pictured below. See page xiv for a complete description of this strand.

Faces and Feelings

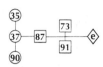

LESSON 38

Human Measurements

Suggested Art Materials

See the art materials list in the student book.

Helpful Teaching Hints

- Show with a tape measure, using a tall student and a short student, that the height of a body does not necessarily affect the basic body proportions.*
- Have students select a part of the body (head, hand, or foot) to use as a basis for measurement. Using the length of the body part as a measuring guide, each student will then measure his or her own body parts to note relationships and proportions. Then have students compare these measurements for sections of the body, such as shoulder to waist, neck to heel, shoulder to fingertips, hip to knee, knee to ankle, and so on. Unique body characteristics, for example, short-waisted or long-waisted forms, may become apparent in this activity, while reinforcing common body proportions, regardless of height.

Additional Materials Needed:
*tape measure ·

Book Strand

Book strand 15, All About People, includes this lesson in its diagram, pictured below. See page xvi for a complete description of this strand.

All About People

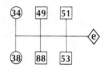

LESSON 39

Different Ways of Drawing

Suggested Art Materials

See the art materials list for this lesson in the student book.

Planning Ahead

Plan on prefacing this lesson with a discussion of the styles of many artists. You may need to research several styles and artists to give students real labels as to eras, techniques, and themes.

Helpful Teaching Hints

- For each piece of art you decide to discuss, lead students to label the style, the theme, the content, and the technique.
- Encourage students to use a medium which they haven't used at all or very little for one of the drawings.
- Review proportions of the human body before students decide on the subject matter.
- Remind students to sketch lightly when creating the preliminary drawing to allow for ease in making changes.
- Discuss the different effects they might obtain using various media before they complete the final drawings.

Book Strand

Book strand 17, The Quest for Self-Expression, includes this lesson in its diagram, pictured below. See page xvi for a complete description of this strand.

The Quest for Self-Expression

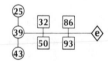

LESSON 40

The Genius of Leonardo da Vinci

Suggested Art Materials

See the art materials list in the student book.

Helpful Teaching Hints

- Use Leonardo da Vinci's *Notebooks* to introduce the students to his curiosity and imagination. Discuss how he, like most artists, included in his work everything he was interested in.*

• Make sure the students understand that studying the work of great artists is valuable in order to understand their techniques, the workings of their minds, and how they viewed life.

Additional Materials Needed:

* *Notebooks* of Leonardo da Vinci

Book Strand

Book strand 3, Artistic Visions, includes this lesson in its diagram, pictured below. See page xiv for a complete description of this strand.

Artistic Visions

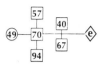

Exploring Art
Keeping a Sketchbook

See pages 12 and 13 for an explanation and teaching suggestions.

Teacher's Notes

Unit III
Composing with Colors

Learning Objectives

In this unit, the students will achieve the following objectives:

Understanding Art

- Understand what color is and how it can be effectively used
- Understand the unique effects different media produce
- Understand effective methods to use when applying different types of media
- Identify and apply important concepts of composition, using color and line

Creating Art

- Apply color effectively, using a variety of media and techniques
- Use brushes to achieve several different effects
- Learn to correctly use paints and brushes, viewfinders, and drawing instruments
- Paint in a variety of styles, creating (among others) realistic, geometric, Impressionistic, and abstract results
- Depict the human body in action

Appreciating Art

- Study and critique various works of well-known artists
- Identify the individual styles and periods of art which are personally most appealing
- Notice color in the environment and how it is affected by light and distance

Unit Strands

A strand consists of a group of related lessons where the student is expected to begin with one of the lesson choices available on the far left (arranged vertically), complete it, proceed horizontally to the next group of choices, make a choice and complete the lesson, and so forth, until the entire sequence has been completed. (See page v for complete instructions on using strands.) The unit strands for this unit are diagrammed at the top of the next column.

Strand G: Color and Composition

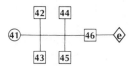

Strand H: Styles of Painting

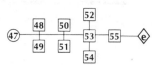

Background Information

Unit III, Composing with Colors, builds on basic skills and experiences developed in the drawing lessons, introducing refinements in color manipulation, more advanced concepts of composition, the design elements of geometric and abstract art, and the creative exploration of styles of painting. On completing these lessons, students will have an increased awareness of style. They will also show progress in the mastery of line, form, design, and composition, brought about by their experiments with using color in an expanded variety of media.

Color is introduced in Lesson 41, the first lesson of the unit. The characteristics of color are defined, and the students are given free reign to experiment with colors to create a design. The medium of watercolors is also introduced in a way that allows students to simply experiment and become comfortable with using the paints.

Lesson 42, Brushing with Rhythm, is a further introduction to paints and brushes; this lesson emphasizes the use of brush strokes to produce a design composed of calligraphic or flowing lines. It is a non-threatening lesson, encouraging fluidity in manual dexterity and spontaneity in use of materials. Keen observation of natural rhythmic forms is important here, reinforcing the students' observational skills. Subtle strengthening of the visual, mental, and manual connections necessary for successful painting experiences is also a part of this lesson.

Lesson 43 continues in the mode of simple introduction with allowance for experimentation. Students improve their skills with watercolors, while having fun combining the paints with wax. The students also learn an important trait of watercolors (they are transparent) through demonstrated results.

Lesson 44, A Watercolor Painting, introduces new painting techniques for using watercolors, while simultaneously introducing the medium of tempera paint. By pointing out the differences between the two media, the lesson draws students to conclude that watercolors are the better medium for painting landscapes. Thus, this lesson builds on the introductory lessons in terms of knowledge gained about technique, usefulness, and properties of watercolors.

Lesson 45, Shapes without Outlines, serves as a starting point for the lessons on composition included in this unit. It is designed to help students conceptualize space as form. It requires students to rearrange their visual impressions, thereby freeing themselves from the habit of focusing too rigidly on objects and their outlines. By painting still lifes, students learn to respond to the unity of the total arrangement and the relationships of the objects to each other. They also learn to actualize the negative space around objects as parts of the composition.

Lesson 46, Viewfinder Pictures, further explores composition by introducing a compositional tool (the viewfinder) used by photographers and painters. An extension of lesson 45, this lesson teaches students to make choices that will lead to interesting compositions. Students also learn the power of discrimination; by selectively leaving out elements, they learn to make their paintings more effective.

Lesson 47, From Dark to Light, reinforces prior drawing lessons in linear perspective and is an extension of composition lessons 45 and 46. Color is also explored again when the concept of atmospheric perspective is introduced. Students are asked to combine color and composition to create the illusion of distance in a painting.

Lesson 48, Bright Blobs and Splashes, begins a more in-depth exploration of painting techniques by exhibiting successful painters' works. Specifically, painting in the Impressionistic manner is introduced, with emphasis placed on how sunlight transforms color. The works of well-known French Impressionists are used both to stimulate students and to guide them in experimenting with the use of color and different brush techniques.

Lesson 49, Paint with Matisse, is an expansion of the previous lesson, using the work of Matisse for inspiration in terms of his use of line, form, rhythm, and color. Since the students have already experimented with these techniques, they can appreciate Matisse's efforts. Experiencing Matisse's approach to his art also helps students to become aware of the diversity and creativity of the style, concept, and use of media that one artist may exemplify in his or her lifetime.

Lesson 50, People at Work, provides students with the conceptual and compositional challenge of painting a picture of a person at work. They are encouraged to develop a sense of suitability in selecting a subject and in deciding how to pose or depict the subject effectively. This lesson creates an awareness of continuity in art, of a long history of genre paintings that show people at work.

Lesson 51, Showing Action in Sports, presents a similar challenge to that of the previous lesson, with more stress on action. It is intended to pique the students' interest, while requiring some level of sophistication in the depiction of proportion and in the use of suitable paints and techniques.

Lesson 52, Geometry in Art, again requires some measure of sophistication, as it presents students with a problem-solving lesson frame similar to that which artists face. Students are limited by the shapes and colors which they can use, and must manage to create a satisfactory design within these strictures.

Lesson 53, Losing Your Head, and Lesson 54, Guess What It Was, are designed to introduce students to the concept of abstract design. Losing Your Head provides a formalized method for creating an abstraction from a realistic object, incorporating the use of line, form, and color. This exercise is expanded in Guess What It Was, which requires students to create abstractions from more complicated forms and then verbalize about the process.

Lesson 55, In Search of a Painting Style, offers students choices in selecting a style in which to create a final painting for this unit. This final product should reveal a maturing discrimination in terms of style and improved mastery of new techniques and media.

Strategies for Motivation

Unit III builds on the basic skills and artistic concepts developed in the drawing unit, but it further expands students' abilities by introducing more complex techniques in different color media and more sophisticated approaches to design and composition. Lessons alternate between having students find creative solutions to design problems and encouraging students to give a free-flowing, spontaneous response.

Activities that will add excitement to the more restricted lessons and play upon the "fun" nature of other lessons are listed below. (See individual lesson guides for specific applications.)

- Bring a big bunch of balloons to class or invite a clown to model for lessons that stress color.
- Use the students' "Geometry in Art" designs for book covers, a classroom logo, or the basis for a board game.
- Play sweeping, flowing music in the background for the "Brushing with Rhythm" lesson.
- Invite a local watercolor artist to demonstrate techniques for the class.
- Go outside to view the effect of sunlight on objects.
- As a class, paint a Matisse-like mural.
- Invite students' relatives to model in their work clothes, the more exotic the better.
- Mount photos and abstractions side-by-side for a bulletin board display.

Extending Art

Exploring Art

This Exploring Art feature integrates art skills with English composition and research skills. It directs the students to use both an art museum and a library to find material for biographies of artists. Begin by explaining that each biography should include three things: historical data about the artist's life, a brief analysis of the artist's style, and the student's personal response to the artist's work. Refer the students to their English texts for information on research writing, and direct them in using the biography section of the library. Possible extensions of the Exploring Art feature include the following:

- Organize a field trip to an art museum. Encourage the students to bring notebooks to jot down names of artists and artworks that interest them. Allow time for the students to capture in free writing their responses to what they see. These notes can later be incorporated into their papers.
- Ask each student to create a piece of art in the style of the artist he or she has chosen to write about.

Additional Activities

Lessons in this unit may be expanded in a number of ways to enhance their creative learning potential and to provide additional motivation to students. Following are a few suggestions along these lines, but you should see the individual lesson guides for specific applications.

- Parades, carnivals, and circuses provide stimuli for lessons on color.
- Have students paint clown faces on one another to show the use of abstract design and color.
- Visit a construction site or some other interesting place to observe people at work.
- Arrange a still life that employs objects of only one color against a similarly colored background.
- Have students design toys, spaceships, or futuristic houses, using only geometric forms.
- Hold class outside on a sunny day. Ask the students to sit under a tree and look up; then have them try to draw and paint the effect of sunlight on the leaves.
- Have students read about their favorite Impressionist painters and then write and share reports about them.

Evaluating Procedures

As noted in the introduction to this book, evaluation in art classes poses unique problems for the teacher. (See pages vii–viii.) The Learning Outcomes address the need for self-evaluation and tests the students on the details of what they have learned. However, the teacher still needs some means of determining the extent of a student's application of specifics to a solid core of basic art knowledge. Three things are involved in this type of evaluation:

1. A written test of the student's recall of important facts
2. An examination of the student's artwork in terms of the achievement of certain previously stated goals
3. An oral discussion with the student involving his or her comments on a particular piece of art

These three evaluative components for Unit III are explained below.

Vocabulary

Students who complete this unit should be able to define and correctly use the art terms listed below and on the following page. A written test on the unit should, then, be based on these terms.

abstract	composition
analogous colors	cool colors
atmospheric	foreground
perspective	hue
background	Impressionist
center of interest	intensity
color	landscape

complementary colors	linear perspective
compose	media
opaque	style
pigment	tempera
portrait	tint
primary colors	tone
proportion	transparent
realistic	unified
resist	unity
rhythm	value
secondary colors	viewfinder
shade	warm colors
still life	wash
studio	watercolor

Skills

The artworks students create in this unit should meet the standards listed below. Be certain that the students are aware of these standards both as they plan and as they work. You may choose to keep the list posted throughout the time spent on this unit.

- A variety of media and painting tools are used to achieve certain effects.
- Intensive colors are used for emphasis, and subdued colors are used for subordination.
- Colors are associated with mood and effectiveness rather than with stereotypes.
- The effects of light and distance are shown by the use of colors.
- The composition is enhanced by the effective use of foreground, background, and selective vision.
- The painting reveals an individual style.

Application of Knowledge

Listening to a student talk about an artwork can give you a true sense of how much the student understands the basic elements and principles of design. However, the planning behind such a discussion is important. First, the work to be discussed must be chosen in advance and studied by the teacher. Questions must be written that will lead the student into the correct areas of emphasis. Last, the discussion should be arranged to take place on a one-to-one basis so that the more reticent students are not left out of a group discussion.

An effective discussion for this unit can stem from comparing and contrasting a realistic and an abstract interpretation of the same subject. Suggested artworks to use for this purpose are *Fishing Boats Offshore in a Calm* by Willem van de Velde (realistic) and *Blue Sails* by Lyonel Feininger (abstract).

Supplementary Materials and Resources

Teacher Resources

Baker, Leslie A. *The Art Teacher's Resource Book.* Reston, Virginia: Reston Publishing Co., Inc., 1979.

An extremely useful basic resource guide, this book includes chapters on drawing, painting, printmaking, crafts of many kinds, photography, and filmmaking. It also covers materials use, care of tools, how-to diagrams and photos, and a bibliography for each chapter.

Bartlett, Adam. *Drawing and Painting the Landscape.* Secaucus, New Jersey: Chartwell Books, Inc., 1982.

This source comprehensively includes drawing with pencil and with pen and ink; using pastels; watercolor, gouache, tempera, oil, and acrylic painting techniques; and a glossary of terms. Excellent black-and-white and color photographs of works in progress are included, along with color samples and instructions for using materials and tools.

Chase, Alice Elizabeth. *Famous Artists of the Past.* New York: Platt and Munk, 1964.

This book includes 27 artists, from Michelangelo and Leonardo da Vinci to the French Impressionists. It contains 177 reproductions, 44 of which are in acceptable color. Several pages of text about each artist include comments on artistic achievements and other biographical information. This source is also suitable for student reading.

————. *Famous Paintings.* New York: Platt and Munk, 1962.

This book is composed of discussions and comparisons of several paintings by different artists, centered around particular themes. There are 52 themes, including Playing Games, Music in Paint, Children and Pets, People Working, Patterns in Color, etc. There are 184 plates in all, 54 in good color reproduction. As with the other Chase book, this one is suitable for students.

Educational Motion Pictures. Bloomington: Audio-Visual Center, Indiana University, 1980.

A number of films on drawing, painting, and artists are included, with supplements to the catalog available.

Goodrich, Lloyd. *Three Centuries of American Art.*
    New York: Fredrick A. Prager, 1966.
This is a pictorial survey showing works of leading figures from the past and present. (It gives about equal emphasis to 20th-century art and art of the past.) It is a well-written text with 130 illustrations, 40 in excellent color.

Simon, Matila. *The Shorewood Art Reference Guide,*
    Revised, 3rd ed. New York: Shorewood
    Reproductions, Inc., 1970.
This is a catalog of black-and-white photos of prints available from Shorewood, each accompanied by a brief description. A longer essay on each artist is also included. Master artists from the Italian Renaissance to 20th-century American art are covered, with Oriental and Mexican art included. Also provided are series on the use of color, line, shape, balance, composition, etc.

Slide Buyer's Guide, 4th ed. Mid-America College Art
    Association Visual Resource Committee. Kan-
    sas City: University of Missouri, 1980.

Stern, Arthur. *How to See Color and Paint It.* New
    York: Watson-Guptill Publications, 1984.
Based on the "color spot" method of Charles Hawthorne, this book is designed to train the eye to see true colors. Simple illustrated color exercises, painted with a palette knife, are adaptable to classroom use.

Student Resources

Llobera, José. *Alive to Art: Portraying People and
    Places.* New York: Crane, Russak and Co., Inc.,
    1976.
This is one of a series, translated from Spanish, which includes *Exploring Color and Crafts* and *Subjects and Skills.* These are large format books, illustrated with colorful drawings, photos and sketches showing how-to, and reproductions by famous artists. Instructions on design, drawing, painting, and a large variety of three-dimensional crafts are included. This series is a real inspiration for teachers and students.

Raboff, Ernest. *Picasso.* Garden City, New York: Dou-
    bleday and Co., 1978.
Books in this series include those about Klee, Chagall, Renoir, and Van Gogh, all useful for this unit on painting. They are short, colorful, vibrant, and whimsical—very appealing to youngsters.

TEACHING SUGGESTIONS
for Lessons 41–55

LESSON 41
Colorful Creations

Suggested Art Materials
See the art materials list for this lesson in the student book.

Planning Ahead
Bring a bunch of floating balloons, beach balls, umbrellas, or flowers to class to provide focus on colors.
Additional Materials Needed:
colorful objects

Helpful Teaching Hints

- Discuss with students their color preferences. See if each student can label himself or herself a "warm" or "cool" person.
- If possible, bring paint or carpet samples of many colors to class. See if students can differentiate between warm and cool colors.
- Refer students to page 3 of the student book for further information on color.
Additional Materials Needed:
* carpet samples

Book Strands
Book strand 6, Enjoying Color, and book strand 11, Imagineering, include this lesson in their diagrams, pictured below. See pages xiv and xv, respectively, for complete descriptions of these strands.

Enjoying Color   Imagineering

LESSON 42
Brushing with Rhythm

Suggested Art Materials
See the art materials list for this lesson in the student book.

Planning Ahead

Assemble reproductions of Oriental, European, and American work which exemplify the use of flowing or calligraphic lines. Show that these artists were using similar media, and explain that, though their styles differ, they all reveal mastery in the use of the rhythmic line.

Additional Materials Needed:

prints or slides of Oriental, European, and American calligraphic work

Helpful Teaching Hints

- Play recorded music or nature sounds that are rhythmic—the sound of water flowing, the ebb and flow of the surf, the wind sighing in the trees, the roll of thunder, bird songs.*
- Invite a dance student or mime to demonstrate flowing movements, and have the students imitate the movements to music.
- Hang large pieces of transparent fabric or strips of colored paper from the ceiling, and then turn on a fan to create movement.**
- Have students observe a fish or snake to take note of its flowing movements.***

Additional Materials Needed:

  * records: music, sounds from nature

 ** strips of fabric or paper, fan

*** fish or snake

Book Strands

Book strand 8, Studying Lines, and book strand 21, Artists and Art Styles, include these lessons in their diagrams, pictured below. See pages xiv and xvii, respectively, for a complete description of these strands.

Studying Lines   Artists and Art Styles

LESSON 43

Painting over Wax

Suggested Art Materials

See the art materials list for this lesson in the student book.

Helpful Teaching Hints

Supervise the students' mixing of watercolors, point-

ing out that the thinner the paint is, the more translucent the effect will be.

Book Strand

Book strand 17, The Quest for Self-Expression, includes this lesson in its diagram, pictured below. See page xvi for a complete description of this strand.

The Quest for Self-Expression

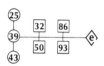

LESSON 44

A Watercolor Painting

Suggested Art Materials

See the art materials list for this lesson in the student book. Note: Drawing boards are almost a necessity for this lesson. Large masonite panels may be cut to suitable sizes.

Helpful Teaching Hints

- Invite a watercolor artist to demonstrate paper stretching, putting on a wash, and developing a painting.
- Explain the meaning of the terms *opaque* and *transparent* by using sheets of stained glass.*
- Show or display slides or pictures of well-known watercolor artists.**

Materials Needed:

  * sheets of opaque and transparent stained glass

** slides or pictures by watercolor artists

Book Strand

Book strand 12, The Look of Distance, includes this lesson in its diagram, pictured below. See page xv for a complete description of this strand.

The Look of Distance

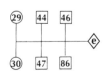

LESSON 45

Shapes Without Outlines

Suggested Art Materials

See the art materials list in the student book.

Planning Ahead

The object of this lesson is to help students unfocus on outlines or contours of objects, thereby visualizing a unified composition. They should learn and understand that space between, behind, and around objects is also a form. One way to achieve this is to have students paint a still life in shades of gray, black, and white. Another is to arrange a still life with objects and backdrop all of one color.

Additional Materials Needed:
still life objects, backdrop of cloth or paper (all one color)

Helpful Teaching Hints

- Use still life objects with less distinct forms or outlines—fuzzy balls or toys; cotton balls; fluffy towels; mounds of flour, sugar, sand, potting soil.*
- Have the students fill the background first, working toward defining object shapes from behind and around, and demonstrating an awareness of negative shapes between objects.
- Show a variety of works by Monet, Manet, Degas, Cézanne, and Turner to show how artists approach this problem in their work.**

Additional Materials Needed:
 * still life objects with indistinct forms
** pictures by Monet, Manet, Degas, Cézanne, Turner

Book Strand

Book strand 1, Thinking with Contours, includes this lesson in its diagram, pictured below. See page xiii for a complete description of this strand.

Thinking with Contours

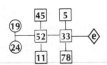

LESSON 46

Viewfinder Pictures

Suggested Art Materials

See the art materials list for this lesson in the student book.

Planning Ahead

To help students recognize a good composition when they see it, and to help them discriminate between what should be added and what should be left out,

arrange frames on the classroom windows. With black paint or tape, create a variety of rectangular shapes at different heights on the glass, or hang real picture frames at different heights. Ask the students to choose those frames enclosing the best compositions and tell why.

Additional Materials Needed:
black tape or picture frames

Helpful Teaching Hints

- Have students compose their scenes on a felt board. They should start with many felt shapes, removing and rearranging them until they are satisfied with the composition.*
- Go outside with large frames or viewfinders to find land/streetscape compositions to paint. Nail the frames to long stakes, if possible, to poke into the ground so the frames will stay in place while the students paint scenes. Have the student use broad-tipped felt markers for quick results.**

Additional Materials Needed:
 * felt board, many colorful felt shapes
** frames, viewfinders, wooden stakes, felt tip markers

Related Art Careers (photographer and filmmaker)

The works of photographer Ansel Adams displayed in art galleries and assembled in books confirm photography as a major artform. Photography is now taught in many design colleges, and includes a combination of basic art courses, liberal arts, and training in the technology of the camera.

Have students look through a variety of different professional photographs, noting specific features, such as the composition, lighting, angle of the camera, or message that is conveyed.

A new, related field is that of filmmaking. Because it is costly and highly technical, the nature of the art is unique. Education might include courses in video, cinematography, graphic design, and photography. Fine arts, make-up, and history of costuming and drama are also helpful. There is great demand for filmmakers outside the major film industry in such fields as education, industry sales and training, commercials, and computer graphics.

Have students watch an educational or commercial video and critique the artistic aspects of the film.

Book Strands

Book strand 9, Composing Pictures and Designs, and book strand 12, The Look of Distance, include this lesson in their diagrams, pictured at the top of the next column. See page xv for complete descriptions of these strands.

Composing Pictures and Designs   The Look of Distance

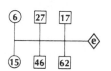 

LESSON 47

From Dark to Light

Suggested Art Materials

See the art materials list in the student book.

Planning Ahead

Exhibit examples of students' landscape pencil drawings, covering them with sheets of colored, transparent acetate, to help illustrate the use of color in defining distance. Have the students paint the darker areas, directly on the acetate, with opaque paints.
Additional Materials Needed:
colored, transparent acetate

Helpful Teaching Hints

Use reproductions of paintings by Russell, Remington, and Monet, or photographs featuring misty, foggy, cloudy scenes, to stimulate the students.
Additional Materials Needed:
photographs/reproductions by Russell, Remington, Monet

Book Strand

Book strand 12, The Look of Distance, includes this lesson in its diagram, pictured below. See page xv for a complete description of this strand.

The Look of Distance

LESSON 48

Bright Blobs and Splashes

Suggested Art Materials

See the art materials list for this lesson in the student book.

Planning Ahead

Show slides or films about the French Impressionists, contrasting their work with prior examples of French painting. Explain that these artists influenced and stimulated one another's work by discussing together their theories and paintings, exhibiting together, etc., so that the body of their work formed a "school of Impressionistic art."
Additional Materials Needed:
slides, film projector

Helpful Teaching Hints

- Paint outside on a sunny day, asking students to produce pictures of sunlight through leaves or on water, or to paint still lifes of colorful flowers and fruits on a sunny window ledge.*
- Play French songs or tunes as background music.**
- Exhibit a selection of Impressionist paintings, with brief quotes by each painter about his or her work. Then have the students write brief statements about their own work to exhibit with their paintings.***

Additional Materials Needed:
  * colorful flowers and fruits
 ** records/tapes of French music, phonograph or recorder
*** reproductions of Impressionists' paintings, typed statements quoting them about their work

Book Strand

Book strand 6, Enjoying Color, includes this lesson in its diagram, pictured below. See page xiv for a complete description of this strand.

Enjoying Color

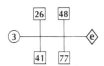

LESSON 49

Paint with Matisse

Suggested Art Materials

See the art materials list for this lesson in the student book.

Planning Ahead

Show slides or reproductions of Matisse's work, including examples of a variety of his styles. Plan with your students a series of paintings incorporating a number of his themes, techniques, and uses of

media, and showing the progression of his work.
Additional Materials Needed:
slides, projector, reproductions of Matisse's work

Helpful Teaching Hints

- Exhibit the types of Japanese prints which influenced Matisse and other Impressionists.*
- Arrange a still life using Japanese objects, furniture, or fabrics, as Matisse might have.**
- Plan a large wall mural in the Matisse style, using flowing lines and colorful cutouts.***

Additional Materials Needed:
   * Japanese prints
  ** Japanese objects
*** mural-sized paper, colored paper for cutouts (Note: Banner or mural-sized paper is available in bright colors.)

Book Strands

Book strand 3, Artistic Visions, and book strand 15, All About People, include this lesson in their diagrams, pictured below. See pages xiv and xvi, respectively, for complete descriptions of these strands.

Artistic Visions

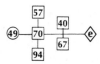

All About People

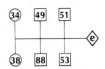

LESSON 50

People at Work

Suggested Art Materials

See the art materials list for this lesson in the student book.

Planning Ahead

Display reproductions of famous paintings which show people at work: paintings by Vermeer, Courbet, Daumier, Hals, Rivera, or Rockwell. Contrast these with current paintings and/or photographs, discussing how types of work have changed and how the style of depicting people at work has or has not changed. Have students list the kinds of work which they would like to portray people doing and why.
Additional Materials Needed:
reproductions of paintings by Vermeer, Courbet, Daumier, Hals, Rivera, Rockwell; photographs showing people at work.

Helpful Teaching Hints

- Ask the students to focus on a relative or friend who has a sense of pride and responsibility about his or her work. Have them discuss how they will each compose a picture showing this person at work.
- With your class, visit a construction site, shopping mall, supermarket, farm, or harbor, asking the students to make quick sketches of people at work.
- Bring specific work tools to class, and ask the students to imagine someone using them and then to compose a painting dramatizing their use.*

Additional Materials Needed:
* tools

Book Strand Lesson

Book strand 17, The Quest for Self-Expression, includes this diagram in its strand, pictured below. See page xvi for a complete description of this strand.

The Quest for Self-Expression

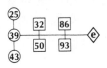

LESSON 51

Showing Action in Sports

Planning Ahead

Collect photographs of athletes in action for students to scrutinize. (*Sports Illustrated*, newspaper sports sections, and sports books are good sources.) Plan time for students to observe and sketch people participating in various sports.
Additional Materials Needed:
* photos of athletes in action

Helpful Teaching Hints

Discuss with the students what kinds of sports activities could be depicted well with watercolors (graceful sports like diving, and sports like hang gliding or snow skiing that occur in pastel environments), and what kinds of activities might require tempera paints for accurate depictions (strenuous sports such as weightlifting, and sports occurring in bright environments).

Book Strand

Book strand 15, All About People, includes this

lesson in its diagram, pictured below. See page xvi for a complete description of this strand.

All About People

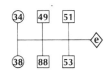

LESSON 52

Geometry in Art

Suggested Art Materials

See the art materials list for this lesson in the student book.

Planning Ahead

Help the students focus on how much of our environment is composed of geometrical forms. Use colored tape to outline several geometrical shapes in the classroom (bulletin boards, fish tank, globe, etc.), and then have the students see how many different shapes they can find.
Additional Materials Needed:
colored tape

Helpful Teaching Hints

- Use drawing boards, if possible, pointing out that they are essential tools for many kinds of artwork.
- Display pictures by Mondrian, Alber, and Rothko to show how painters use geometric forms in their work.*
- Display ships' flags, heraldic devices, Pop art calendars, or book and record jackets to show how graphic artists utilize geometric forms in their work.**

Additional Materials Needed:
  * pictures by Mondrian, Alber, Rothko, others
** flags, Pop art calendars, book or record covers

Safety Precautions

Provide corks to put on sharp compass points when they are not in use.

Book Strands

Book strand 1, Thinking with Contours, and book strand 13, Artistic Surprises, include this lesson in their diagrams, pictured at the top of the next column. See pages xiii and xv, respectively, for complete descriptions of these strands.

Thinking with Contours   Artistic Surprises

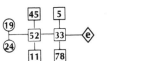

LESSON 53

Losing Your Head

Suggested Art Materials

See the art materials list for this lesson in the student book.

Planning Ahead

Show slides of reproductions of works by Picasso, Dubuffet, Leger, Klee, Chagall, and Miró. Have the students discover and identify abstracted objects in these works. Then ask the students if they can relate their dreams, quick glimpses from a car window, or things seen in a lightning storm to these abstractions. How would they paint their own experiences in this way?
Additional Materials Needed:

slides, projector; reproductions of works by Picasso, Dubuffet, Leger, Klee, Chagall, and Miró.

Helpful Teaching Hints

- Explain abstraction as an imaginative way of creating other dimensions of reality.
- Have the students produce a stained glass design, based on an abstraction of a real object, using colored transparent acetate and black ink.*
- Have the students cut up, in horizontal or vertical strips or in puzzle-like pieces, large magazine photographs of people and objects. Then have them rearrange the pieces and glue them on a sheet of paper in a way that conveys the original message of the photo.**

Additional Materials Needed:
  * colored transparent acetate, black ink
 ** large magazines, paper cutter, scissors, paper, glue

Book Strands

Book strand 11, Imagineering, and book strand 15, All About People, include this lesson in their diagrams. See pages xv and xvi, respectively, for complete descriptions of these strands.

Imagineering 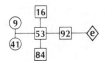 All About People 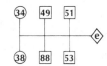 Abstract Puzzles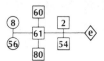

LESSON 54

Guess What It Was

Suggested Art Materials

See the art materials list for this lesson in the student book.

Planning Ahead

This lesson is a continuation of Lesson 53, and the suggestions listed there may be utilized here as well. In addition to the van Doesburg illustration in the text, works by Picasso, Braque, Cézanne, and Feininger show how artists arrive at abstractions, using real objects and street, land, and seascapes for inspiration.

Additional Materials Needed:

slides, projector; reproductions of works by Picasso, Braque, Cézanne, Feininger

Helpful Teaching Hints

• Have students read about and report on American abstract artists, so they will realize there has been a continuity in the use of abstraction as an art form.

• Encourage students to use as much shading as possible to create the realistic first drawing. The shaded areas can become guides for creating abstract shapes within the body of the subject.

• Have students compare the simple, stylized art forms of past civilizations with modern abstract art. Ask them to discuss any influences they can see.

• To expand this lesson or to help those students who have difficulty visualizing the underlying abstract shapes in their realistic drawing, have them create an artwork in reverse; by starting with a few basic geometric shapes, they can create an image of an animal, bird, or person and then add details to make the subject realistic.

Book Strand

Book strand 2, Abstract Puzzles, includes this lesson in its diagram, pictured at the top of the next column. See page xiii for a complete description of this strand.

LESSON 55

In Search of a Painting Style

Suggested Art Materials

See the art materials list for this lesson in the student book.

Planning Ahead

Present a slide show reviewing works by the artists covered in this unit. Make available prints, color reproductions, art history books, and art magazines for browsing through. Remind the students that an artist's style is as unique as each person's handwriting and that they should be careful when choosing a particular style to imitate. This style should be one they are comfortable with and one which best expresses their individual points of view and abilities.

Additional Materials Needed:

slides, projector, color reproductions, art history books, art magazines

Helpful Teaching Hints

• Discuss with each student individually the elements of style which attract him or her to a particular artist's work. Also discuss subject selection and choice of media to be used.

• Have the students make a number of rough sketches before doing their final work.

• Show the students how to mat, mount, label, and exhibit their final work.*

• Arrange to have an exhibit of your students' work displayed in a prominent school or community location. Have the students prepare the publicity, put up the exhibit, arrange a reception for the opening (if possible), and be prepared to discuss their work with guests. Display a print by the artist each student selected to imitate alongside his or her project.

Additional Materials Needed:

* mat board or illustration board (white or off-white), mat knives, paper cutter, tape, pins or tacks (for mounting)

Safety Precautions

Mat knives need to be very sharp and have their blades in securely in order to cut effectively. Show the students how to change the blades safely. Instruct the students to place corks on the blades and put the knives in drawers or labeled boxes when they are not in use. Put bright tape on the knives' handles so they are easily seen among a pile of papers.

Book Strand

Book strand 10, Ideas from Other Cultures, includes this lesson in its diagram, pictured at the top of the next column. See page xv for a complete description of this strand.

Ideas from Other Cultures

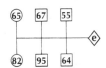

Exploring Art

A Painter's Biography

See page 23 for an explanation and teaching suggestions.

Teacher's Notes

Unit IV
Sculpting and Forming

Learning Objectives

In this unit, the students will achieve the following objectives:

Understanding Art

• Recognize the inherent artistic characteristics of natural and man-made objects
• Understand the influence of ancient cultures on the history of art
• Understand the use of simple techniques and tools in molding, modeling, and carving to create reliefs and three-dimensional sculptural forms

Creating Art

• Make simple constructions out of found materials
• Make simple architectural drawings and models
• Use ancient art styles to create their own artworks
• Use various art materials and tools to sculpt and form artistic pieces

Appreciating Art

• Discuss useful techniques and materials for creating three-dimensional art forms, and evaluate their results
• Talk about art in the environment—its beauty and its function

Unit Strands

A strand consists of a group of related lessons where the student is expected to begin with one of the lesson choices available on the far left (arranged vertically), complete it, proceed horizontally to the next group of choices, make a choice and complete the lesson, and so forth, until the entire sequence has been completed. (See page v for complete instructions on using strands.) The unit strands for this unit are diagramed below and at the top of the next column.

Strand I: Sculpture, Molds, and Casts

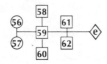

Strand J: Carving, Modeling, and Molding

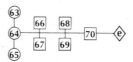

Background Information

Modeling, carving, and constructing are three of the art activities that teach students fundamental concepts of form and function. Through these activities, students learn to see the structures of objects around them. They observe sculpture and three-dimensional forms as part of their built environment.

As the students go through the lessons in Unit IV, Sculpting and Forming, they learn to become observant about shapes and forms created by common, everyday objects. The very first lesson, Sculpture from Found Objects, instructs the students to find objects in the natural environment to use in their art. The following lesson, Redesigning Nature, builds on this concept of creating art out of nature. In fact, every lesson in this unit instructs the students to closely observe their environment, whether it be natural or man-made, to find artistic materials or to notice inherent artistic characteristics. Students learn to appreciate everything from buildings to trees as having artistic form.

Hand-in-hand with instructions to closely observe the surroundings are instructions on how to create art forms. Students learn in the early lessons of the unit to join found three-dimensional objects together to form sculptures. Then they work toward actually constructing the elements to be joined together— from cardboard shapes in Lesson 58 and Lesson 59 to pieces of clay in Lesson 68. These joining lessons culminate in the architecture lessons at the end of the unit, lessons that require creativity as well as skill and artistic vision.

The more sophisticated sculpting and molding lessons appear in the middle of the unit. Lesson 61, Handwarming Sculpture, is a non-threatening introduction to these lessons. It concentrates on letting students simply become comfortable with the medium of plaster of paris so that they can effectively use it in Lesson 62. Lesson 65 serves as a similar introduction to the medium of clay. It is a simple but interesting lesson that leads students easily into more advanced uses of clay in Lessons 64–67. These clay lessons culminate with Lesson 68, Slab Buildings.

As is usual for this book, lessons on ancient cultures and their art forms are introduced, both to give students models to follow and to instill in them the important feeling of the continuity of art throughout history. The featured pictures of important artworks contribute to the visual experience the students must have in this unit to understand and create objects with definite artistic forms and shapes.

Strategies for Motivation

Students like to relate what they do with what they see around them. Bringing actual pieces of three-dimensional work into the classroom for discussion and appreciation can be a very effective introduction to the making of sculptural forms. Below are suggestions for putting students directly in touch with actual artworks. (See individual lesson guides for specific applications.)

- Bring in visuals of Egyptian and African art.
- Bring in samples of three-dimensional works. Allow the students to handle and feel these samples; the feeling of form reinforces the concept of three dimensions.
- Involve students in the bringing of samples. This will provide them with the personal experience of identifying and selecting examples that are truly representative of what is being studied, while also demonstrating for you whether or not they understand exactly what each art form is.
- Spend time discussing man-made environmental art, using buildings in everyone's frame of reference as examples of styles and functional traits.

Extending Art

Exploring Art

This feature encourages the students to draw on their imaginations, their knowledge in the fields of mathematics and geography, and their sensitivity to natural forms by having them design bridges that fit the land around them. The students are directed to observe many kinds of bridges, choose the areas (either real or imaginary) their bridges will span, sketch the areas, and then design their bridges. Provide slides, books, encyclopedias, or copies of such magazines as *National Geographic* with illustrations of bridges

in various countries and settings. Ask to see the students' sketches of their settings before they begin the bridge designs. Suggestions for extending this Exploring Art feature include the following:

- Students might enjoy reading literary works dealing with bridges (*Bridge to Terabithia*, *The Bridge of San Luis Rey*, the Norse mythology featuring a rainbow bridge) and basing their bridge designs on what they have read. Students who design bridges for imaginary settings may want to compose poems or short stories to accompany their designs.
- Some students may enjoy constructing models of their designs. Encourage them to choose their media creatively: wire, toothpicks, thread, popsicle sticks, plaster of paris are all possibilities.

Additional Activities

Visits to museums and art galleries to see how different sculptors express their ideas through various media will help to make the students' learning more meaningful and exciting. It is useful for the teacher to have a preview of the exhibits to be seen on such outings, however, so that he or she can guide the discussion on the actual visits. Other suggestions include:

- Plan field trips to community centers and places of interest where sculptures are displayed.
- Visit a sculptor's studio, or have local artists come to your class to display their works and give talks and demonstrations.
- Ask the students to make sketches of natural and man-made objects that catch their attention. These can be used as resource materials for future lessons.

Evaluating Procedures

As noted in the introduction to this book, evaluation in art classes poses unique problems for the teacher. (see pages vii–viii.) The Learning Outcomes address the need for self-evaluation and test the students on the details of what they have learned. However, the teacher still needs some means of determining the extent of a student's application of specifics to a solid core of basic art knowledge. Three things are involved in this type of evaluation:

1. A written test of the student's recall of important facts.
2. An examination of the student's artwork in terms of the achievement of certain previously stated goals

3. An oral discussion with the student involving his or her comments on a particular piece of art

These three evaluative components for Unit IV are explained below.

Vocabulary

Students who complete this unit should be able to define and correctly use the art terms listed below. A written test on the unit should, then, be based on these terms.

abstract	rasp
additive sculpture	relief
architect	score
armature	sculpture
assemblage	slab
carve	slip
cast	slot
chisel	slotting
clay	statue
dimension	style
functional	subtractive sculpture
imagery	tab
mallet	theme
mold	theme and variations
mural	three-dimensional
papier-mâché	unified
plane	wedging

Skills

The artworks students create in this unit should meet the standards listed below. Be certain that the students are aware of these standards both as they plan and as they work. You may choose to keep the list posted throughout the time spent on this unit.
• The artwork is successful from all angles.
• The composition reveals balance and unity.
• Different textures are juxtaposed to create interest.

Application of Knowledge

Listening to a student talk about an artwork can give you a true sense of how much the student understands the basic elements and principles of design. However, the planning behind such a discussion is important. First, the work to be discussed must be chosen in advance and studied by the teacher. Questions must be written that will lead the student into the correct areas of emphasis. Last, the discussion should be arranged to take place on a one-to-one basis so that the more reticent students are not left out of a group discussion.

Suggested sculptures that students will enjoy discussing are *Great Anteater* by Erwin Springweiler and *The Snake* by Isamu Noguchi. A modern building that might interest students is the Nakagin Capsule Tower in Tokyo, designed by Kisho Kurokawa.

Supplementary Materials and Resources

Brommer, Gerald F. *Wire Sculpture and Other Three-Dimensional Construction.* Worcester, Mass.: Davis Publications, Inc.

Throughout this book the emphasis is on solving problems that encourage originality and innovation. The use of various media is discussed and illustrated. Papier-mâché and plaster are used in combination with wires to create simple and interesting three-dimensional constructions.

_____, and George F. Horn. *Art: Your Visual Environment.* Wocester, Mass.: Davis Publications, Inc., 1984.

This is an interesting book which gives examples of works in sculpture and architecture, while showing the use of the elements of design in other areas of art.

Hart, Tony. *The Young Designer.* New York and London: Frederick Warne and Co., Inc., 1968.

This book deals with elements and principles of design as applied to three-dimensional work. It is a helpful aid to the study of sculpting and forming processes.

TEACHING SUGGESTIONS for Lessons 56–70

LESSON 56

Sculpture from Found Objects

Suggested Art Materials

See the art materials list for this lesson in the student book.

Planning Ahead

Set up a display corner in the room, to be used throughout the unit. (Have the students help keep it filled with examples relevant to the lessons.) For this first lesson, display examples of assemblage that you can use to help explain the concept.

Additional Materials Needed:
materials for a display corner, examples of assemblage

Helpful Teaching Hints

For these early lessons, encourage the students to create only simple, abstract geometric forms rather than realistic representations.

Safety Precaution

Use glue and spray paints only in a well-ventilated area.

Book Strand

Book strand 2, Abstract Puzzles, includes this lesson in its diagram, pictured below. See page xiii for a complete description of this strand.

Abstract Puzzles

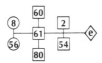

LESSON 57

Redesigning Nature

Suggested Art Materials

See the art materials list for this lesson in the student book.

Planning Ahead

Bring in plants, leaves, grass, etc., and ask the students to bring in some objects from nature, too. Discuss the suggestions of certain imagery evoked by the form, color, texture, and shape of each object.

Helpful Teaching Hints

Open the lesson by referring to the pictures that accompany it. Have the students suggest how they would change the character of each work pictured.

Safety Precautions

Be sure the room is well-ventilated if using strong glue, and that you store it in a safe place away from open flames.

Related Art Career (sculptor)

While pieces of sculpture are becoming more and more common in public places, the art of sculpting is becoming more diverse. Some craftsmen have

turned commercial sculpture into a thriving self-operated business.

A sculptor may be commissioned to create an artwork for the interiors of public buildings such as libraries, banks, malls, and other commercial places, as well as outdoor areas surrounding these buildings. The architectural sculptor needs an awareness of people, a knowledge of interior and exterior space in addition to an interest in architecture. A representative usually handles the business details, but the sculptor should be knowledgeable in this area and also understand the logistics of handling, delivering, and installing large pieces of artwork.

Conduct a discussion with students about the different pieces of sculpture they may have seen in their community or city. Discuss the different media used in these sculptures and the way the artwork fits in with the environment.

Book Strand

Book strand 3, Artistic Visions, includes this lesson in its diagram, pictured below. See page xiv for a complete description of this strand.

Artistic Visions

LESSON 58

Building with Flat Shapes

Suggested Art Materials

See the art materials list for this lesson in the student book.

Planning Ahead

Prepare a set of cardboard shapes of various sizes with slots cut beforehand for demonstration at the beginning of the lesson. Show several forms that can be created by varying the use of the different shapes; then let students experiment with the shapes, too.

Helpful Teaching Hints

- Students may wish to paint their cardboard pieces before slotting them together.
- To help students grasp the idea of different planes intersecting with one another, use these visual aids: show three-dimensional works from various angles, cast flood lights on three-dimensional

works so their planes are more visible, rotate the works on a banding wheel.*

Additional Materials Needed:
* flood lights, banding wheel

Safety Precautions

State two rules for the use of sharp instruments:
(1) Always cut away from the body.
(2) Keep fingers out of the path of cutting tools.

Book Strand

Book strand 4, Art with Flat Planes, includes this lesson in its diagram, pictured below. See page xiv for a complete description of this strand.

Art with Flat Planes

LESSON 59

Bent Sculpture

Suggested Art Materials

See the art materials list for this lesson in the student book.

Helpful Teaching Hints

Spend more time than usual introducing this lesson. Demonstrate scoring by creating different forms through scoring the cardboard in various ways. Then allow plenty of time for the students to experiment with the technique before they embark on a creative effort.

Safety Precautions

Remind the students to make the scoring motions *away* from their bodies, in case they slip or are jolted.

Related Art Career (industrial designer)

Industrial designers are problem solvers. They experiment, explore, and plan designs for products. They combine technical knowledge of methods, materials, and machines with design talent to create or improve both the appearance and function of machine-made products. Part designer, technician, and merchandiser, they work between industry and the consumer to improve our standard of living. A college education combining courses in graphic design, photography, architecture, illustration, engineering, and

crafts will prepare the industrial designer for a diverse career. The initial position for this career is sometimes a model-maker or draftsperson, often called a technical illustrator. Advancing to a designer, one who works on a team in most large firms, requires the ability to work with people and to communicate ideas.

Bring in a collection of products that have been designed by industrial designers, such as a can opener, aluminum can, toothpaste tube, bicycle pump, helmet, or jogging shoes. Discuss the effectiveness of the product design with students. Then have students invent their own industrial designs.

Book Strand

Book strand 4, Art with Flat Planes, includes this lesson in its diagram, pictured below. See page xiv for a complete description of this strand.

Art with Flat Planes

LESSON 60

Theme and Variations

Suggested Art Materials

See the art materials list for this lesson in the student book.

Helpful Teaching Hints

- To make sure the students understand the concept of a theme and its variations, suggest a theme represented by a classroom object and have the students suggest modes of variations.
- Remind the students that the theme they have chosen should remain recognizable throughout the variations. For example, paper cups will still be realized as such, not simply as material to create something totally different.
- A few simple structural changes can be amplified or emphasized by the addition of color. However, remind students to use color sparingly on forms with complex variations.

Safety Precautions

Remind students when using scissors, to always cut away from the body and to use glue in a well-ventilated area. Also, if the students use a stapler, keep fingers out of the path of the staple.

Book Strand

Book strand 2, Abstract Puzzles, includes this lesson in its diagram, pictured below. See page xiii for a complete description of this strand.

Abstract Puzzles

LESSON 61

Handwarming Sculpture

Suggested Art Materials

See the art materials list for this lesson in the student book.

Helpful Teaching Hints

Ask probing questions about the pictures in this lesson. How did the sculptor arrive at a particular form? Why did the artist not develop the form further?

Book Strand

Book strand 2, Abstract Puzzles, includes this lesson in its diagram, pictured below. See page xiii for a complete description of this strand.

Abstract Puzzles

LESSON 62

Sand Casting

Suggested Art Materials

See the art materials list for this lesson in the student book.

Helpful Teaching Hints

Suggest that students use objects that have unique shapes (such as starfish, geometrical blocks, or shoes) so that the castings will produce more detailed results.

Book Strand

Book strand 9, Composing Pictures and Designs, includes this lesson in its diagram, pictured below. See page xv for a complete description of this strand.

Composing Pictures and Designs

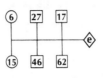

LESSON 63

Alligators, Lions, and Other Wild Beasts

Suggested Art Materials

See the art materials list for this lesson in the student book.

Planning Ahead

Allow plenty of time for this lesson, since students will go from learning about a new art technique and medium to actually using the technique to create a fairly sophisticated final product. Use visual examples to reinforce the concept of relief in sculpture.

Helpful Teaching Hints

- Finished clay pieces should be allowed to dry naturally and completely for several days in a warm place until they no longer feel cold to the touch.
- If the clay is to be fired, be aware that the firing temperature required to mature various types of clay differs. You should select clay and glazes that mature at the same temperature—which may be determined by the capability of your kiln.
- Firing is a two-stage process. Dried clay (sometimes known as "greenware") may be stacked and loaded as closely and tightly as possible for the first firing. This firing will be to approximately cone 015, or 1,500°F, and will bring the clay to a "bisque" stage where it is halfway matured, but still porous enough to absorb liquid glaze.

  Coat the base or foot of bisque ware with commercial *wax resist* or melted paraffin, or simply avoid getting glaze on areas that will touch the kiln shelf. Bisque ware may be glazed either by dipping or pouring the glaze on, or by evenly painting on three coats with a soft brush. Glazed pieces must be loaded into the kiln carefully so they do not touch anything.

Safety Precautions

- Typical firing temperatures for "high fire" clay bodies range from 2,000 to 2,200°F—VERY HOT! A firing kiln should always be supervised to make sure it is operating properly and shuts off when visible "cones" placed in the viewer windows have bent over to indicate that the required temperature has been reached. Students should not be allowed near a hot kiln: clothing can easily be ignited if it touches the kiln, and serious burns are a potential hazard.

- A fired kiln should be allowed to cool naturally for 16 to 24 hours, and should never be opened before it has cooled below at least 500°F. Impatience on this count will result in crazing, tiny networks of cracks in the glaze and clay, which can cause pots to leak or break.

- If you and/or your equipment and materials are new, some experimenting is advisable to discover the most successful combinations of clay types; glaze colors, brands, or formulas; and firing techniques. What takes place inside a firing kiln is really a complicated set of chemical reactions, and because of the large number of variables, some clay bodies will accept some glazes better than others. Glazes may turn out quite differently if fired in a gas or electric kiln; and slight differences in firing temperatures may produce very different effects.

Additional Materials Needed:
*examples of reliefs

Book Strand

Book strand 14, From Observation to Imagination, includes this lesson in its diagram, pictured below. See page xv for a complete description of this strand.

From Observation to Imagination

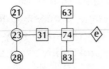

LESSON 64

Modeling and Molding

Suggested Art Materials

See the art materials list for this lesson in the student book.

Helpful Teaching Hints

Helping the students understand the steps of the process they must perform in this lesson will also make it clearer to them why certain limitations are imposed by the media. You may choose, then, to perform the whole process as a demonstration, discussing the steps and media along the way.

Safety Precautions

When using sharp tools, always cut *away* from the body and keep fingers out of the path. Use shellac and paint thinner only in a well-ventilated area.

Book Strand

Book strand 10, Ideas from Other Cultures, includes this lesson in its diagram, pictured below. See page xv for a complete description of this strand.

Ideas from Other Cultures

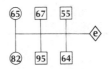

LESSON 65

Ancient Egyptian Art

Suggested Art Materials

See the art materials list for this lesson in the student book.

Planning Ahead

The more visual materials you can gather on ancient Egyptian art, the better. This will help students to better visualize something that is alien to them.
Additional Materials Needed:
examples of ancient Egyptian art

Helpful Teaching Hints

Monitor the students' progress in this lesson, pointing out elements that resemble Egyptian techniques and praising the students for thereby achieving the lesson's objectives.

Safety Precautions

When using sharp tools, always cut *away* from the body and keep fingers out of the path.

Book Strand

Book strand 10, Ideas from Other Cultures, includes this lesson in its diagram, pictured below. See page xv for a complete description of this strand.

Ideas from Other Cultures

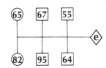

LESSON 66

Hand Sculpture

Suggested Art Materials

See the art materials list for this lesson in the student book.

Planning Ahead

To stimulate the students' sense of touch, prepare a "grab bag" of assorted objects with unique shapes and textures. Have a student grasp an object and try to identify it by feeling it.
Additional Materials Needed:
opaque bag, objects with unique shapes and textures

Helpful Teaching Hints

Further explain the concepts introduced in this chapter, through the use of different terms.
- *Additive sculpture* involves addition to the main form.
- *Subtractive sculpture* involves subtracting what is not wanted from the main form.

Safety Precautions

Remind the students of the two rules for using sharp instruments.
(1) Always cut *away* from the body.
(2) Keep fingers out of the path of cutting tools.

Book Strand

Book strand 7, Exploring Textures, includes this lesson in its diagram, pictured below. See page xiv for a complete description of this strand.

Exploring Textures

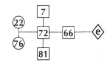

LESSON 67

African Art

Suggested Art Materials

See the art materials list for this lesson in the student book.

Planning Ahead

As was true for Lesson 65, the more visual images of African art you can provide, the better.
Additional Materials Needed:
examples of African art

Helpful Teaching Hints

Give the students the option of experimenting with Picasso's style in their artwork

Safety Precautions

Remind the students to dry their hands before carving, to always cut away from the body when using sharp tools, and to replace the corks on the ends of pointed tools when they are not being used.

Book Strands

Book strand 3, Artistic Visions, and book strand 10, Ideas from Other Cultures, include this lesson in their diagrams, pictured below. See pages xiv and xv, respectively, for complete descriptions of these strands.

Artistic Visions   Ideas from Other Cultures

   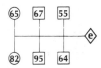

LESSON 68

Slab Buildings

Suggested Art Materials

See the art materials list in the student book.

Planning Ahead

Plan a walking tour of your area, where applicable, along which buildings erected out of slabs can be viewed. Discuss these buildings—their appearances and functional architecture.

Helpful Teaching Hints

- Review the techniques of joining and scoring before the students begin working on their buildings.
- Ask the students to sketch their buildings before they begin making them. This will help them better visualize the role of slabs in their structures.

Safety Precautions

Remind the students to dry their hands before carving and to replace the corks on the ends of pointed tools when they are not being used.

Book Strand

Book strand 4, Art with Flat Planes, includes this lesson in its diagram, pictured below. See page xiv for a complete description of this strand.

Art with Flat Planes

LESSON 69

Buildings Are Like Sculpture

Suggested Art Materials

See the art materials list in the student book.

Planning Ahead

Ask the students in advance to bring building materials from home and to start saving milk cartons or other containers they use at school.

Helpful Teaching Hints

- Spend some time talking about the first paragraph of the lesson. Students' interests are always aroused when they can take part in a discussion about familiar things.
- Discuss individual structural elements of buildings—their purposes and different designs. Refer to specific architectural achievements, such as buildings by Frank Lloyd Wright, to point out the unique ways buildings can be altered.*

Additional Materials Needed:
* pictures of noted architects' buildings

Safety Precautions

Be sure the room is well-ventilated if using strong glue, and that you store it in a safe place away from open flames.

Book Strand

Book strand 16, Being a Designer, includes this lesson in its diagram. See page xvi for a complete description of this strand.

Being a Designer

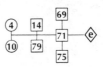

LESSON 70

Being an Architect

Suggested Art Materials

See the art materials list for this lesson in the student book.

Planning Ahead

Collect aerial and street level photographs of buildings to bring to class.
Additional Materials Needed:
various photographs of buildings

Helpful Teaching Hints

Use the photographs you have collected in the following ways:

- Point out that the street level photographs are two-dimensional "models" of the buildings.
- Discuss how the aerial photographs provide a better sense of three dimensions.
- Have the students describe the buildings from the photographs. Which photographs provide the best visual images of three-dimensional form?
- Finally, lead the students to affirm that actual models can give the sense of form that pictures on paper cannot.

Related Art Career (Architect)

A career in architecture requires the most extensive education of all the art-related careers. A sound liberal arts base, including art, technical, and business courses followed by post-graduate work at an architectural school is necessary preparation for obtaining the required license to practice in most states. An architect both designs and supervises construction of buildings. The first step in designing a building is understanding its purpose and the needs of the people who will be using it. The architect must also know zoning laws and all other building codes and regulations for the area. A knowledge of construction materials and methods is also vital in preparing both the interior and exterior design of a building. In addition to the functional aspects of the building, an architect will combine aesthetic features into the design.

For more information, study magazines such as *Architectural Forum* or *Architectural Record*. Have students select a building they particularly like, possibly one from their community, to study and give a short report about its architectural features.

Safety Precautions

When using sharp tools, always cut *away* from the body and keep fingers out of the path.

Book Strand

Book strand 3, Artistic Visions, includes this lesson in its diagram. See page xiv for a complete description of this strand.

Artistic Visions

Exploring Art
Designing a Bridge

See page 33 for an explanation and teaching suggestions.

Teacher's Notes

UNIT V
Working with Ceramics, Crafts, and Textiles

Learning Objectives

In this unit, the students will achieve the following objectives:

Understanding Art

- Understand that artistic objects can be functional and decorative
- Recognize textures of textiles and the different effects they create
- Understand symbols as artistic forms of visual communication

Creating Art

- Use several techniques to create pottery out of clay
- Use a variety of art materials and techniques to create objects to be worn
- Create textiles through stitchery, weaving, and working with yarns and fabrics
- Use symbolism to create communicative designs

Appreciating Art

- Use folk art and other cultures' art traditions for inspiration
- Appreciate the role of communication in art

Unit Strands

A strand consists of a group of related lessons where the student is expectd to begin with one of the lesson choices available on the far left (arranged vertically), complete it, proceed horizontally to the next group of choices, make a choice and complete the lesson, and so forth, until the entire sequence has been completed. (See page v for complete instructions on using strands.) The unit strands for this unit are diagramed below and at the top of the next column.

Strand K: Pottery and Decorative Arts

Strand L: Textiles, Designs, and Symbols

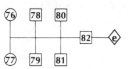

Background Information

The three areas stressed in Unit V—ceramics, crafts, and textiles—are traditionally included in art classes. The reason behind this is a good one: these forms of art are created through the application of basic learned skills and creative craftsmanship. Thus, without requiring too sophisticated a level of skill, lessons centered around these three areas nonetheless require students to work well with different media and to make correct artistic choices about design, color, and purpose. The lessons in this unit follow this pattern by testing the students on skills and knowledge they have previously learned, while also allowing them to see art as functional instead of merely decorative.

The first two lessons in the unit are the ceramic lessons. Ceramics is a practical art form to introduce in the classroom because the malleability of clay makes the creation of three-dimensional forms an achievable task. The first lesson, Clay Coil Pottery, should be introduced properly by a discussion on the historical importance of pottery. You may choose to show the students pictures of pottery from the early civilizations of Egypt, the Middle East, and Greece. Tell the students how archaeologists and curators treasure samples of ancient pottery for the clues they can give us about the ways past civilizations lived. As the students proceed to Lesson 72 and its more sophisticated approach to pottery making, you might extend your discussion of pottery to include the modern tradition in pottery as represented by the works of Bernard Leach and Yamada. Show pictures of some of these works, and discuss the functional and decorative aspects of each.

Students continue in their introduction to functional artworks as they create masks, helmets, hats, and headdresses in Lesson 73 and Lesson 74. These lessons test the students' previously acquired skills and knowledge, while also allowing them a great deal of creative freedom. Lesson 75, Inexpensive Jewelry, continues with this same philosophy; however, this lesson additionally allows the students to practice creating something small and intricate. These three lessons, then, work together to train the students to be exacting as well as creative in their craftsmanship. They also bring art into the personal realm of the students by allowing them to create pieces of art with which they can adorn themselves.

Lessons 76–81 provide the students with experience in various forms of textile art. They learn to create yarn paintings and to design pennants, flags, and banners. They learn the crafts of weaving and stitchery, thereby actually creating their own textiles. Different lessons in this series have different design emphases, of course. Lesson 76 teaches the students to compose designs using the idea of a dominant feature. Lesson 78 and Lesson 79 encourage the students to use symbolism to create communicative artworks. And Lesson 80 centers around the students' developing sense of design and pattern. Still, the basic intention of this series of lessons is to make the students cognizant of the effects created by texture, color, design, and technique in the textiles we see and use every day. This, in turn, leads to a reaffirmation of the important knowledge that art is all around us.

The last lesson in the unit, American Indian Art, introduces the students to a different culture's art forms. At the same time, the lesson confirms for the students that the communicative function of art is a valid and long-lasting one. In this last lesson, the students apply their learned skills, filter through their knowledge about the effects of media and techniques, and use their creativity to decide on and create a project that reflects Indian influences.

Strategies for Motivation

As for the other units, it is a good idea to relate the students' efforts in this unit to what they experience around them. Since the lessons in Unit V teach the students to recognize and appreciate the functional and creative aspects of product design, it is wise to motivate your students to look for these aspects in the objects filling their visual environment. Following are some ways to increase the students' awareness of such elements.

- Ask the students to collect pictures of pottery, masks, headdresses, and jewelry to place in a class scrapbook which the students can use for ideas.

- Set up an art corner where actual samples can be displayed.
- Have the students look through their homes for pieces of commercial pottery that have artistic merit (dishes, planters, etc.). Ask them to bring the objects in for a day-long exhibition. Each object must be accompanied by an index card that titles the piece and describes its particular merits.
- Ask a different student each day to tell about an example of one of the art forms in this unit which he or she has recently encountered. (Examples are pretty fabrics, unusual badges, Boy or Girl Scout merit badges, and interesting masks.)

Extending Art

Exploring Art

In Unit Six, the Exploring Art feature expands the students' knowledge of American Indian cultures while extending their art skills. The feature discusses Sioux artist Black Elk, describes the Plains Indians' pictographic winter-counts drawn on animal hides, and directs the students to draw their own pictographic histories, using Plains Indian art styles. Begin by introducing the term *stylization* and reviewing stylization in both ancient and modern art. Then provide examples of Plains Indian art and ask the students to note styles and recurring motifs. Good sources are such magazines as *National Geographic* and *Smithsonian*; issues of *The Journal of the American Bureau of Ethnography* from the 1800's, carried by most libraries, contain black-and-white photos of winter-count hides. In addition, *Black Elk Speaks*, by John G. Neihardt, contains color reproductions of Black Elk's own drawings as well as telling his story.

- Have a speaker visit the class with artifacts, slides, and/or photos showing the artwork of American Indians of your area. Discuss similarities with, and differences from, Plains Indian art. Make the students aware of the great variety of American Indian art styles.
- Assign students to research in encyclopedias the development of our alphabet from pictographs. Some students may want to develop detailed pictographic communication systems of their own.

Additional Activities

Visits to actual pottery studios, jewelers' shops, and textile factories can greatly enhance the students' experiences with these art forms. Other suggestions for out-of-class activities include the following:

- Visit a museum of art or history to view examples of ancient pottery, jewelry, and textiles.
- Visit a local mall to see modern examples of these art forms. Follow the visit with a discussion of the uniqueness of modern designs. Ask the students how much design depends on function.
- Encourage the students to start their own simple collections of well-designed, functional artworks.

Evaluating Procedures

As noted in the introduction to this book, evaluation in art classes poses unique problems for the teacher. (See pages vi-vii.) The Learning Outcomes address the need for self-evaluation and test the students on the details of what they have learned. However, the teacher still needs some means of determining the extent of a student's application of specifics to a solid core of basic art knowledge. Three things are involved in this type of evaluation:

1. A written test of the student's recall of important facts
2. An examination of the student's artwork in terms of the achievement of certain previously stated goals
3. An oral discussion with the student involving his or her comments on a particular piece of art

These three evaluative components for Unit V are explained below.

Vocabulary

Students who complete this unit should be able to define and correctly use the art terms listed below and at the top of the next column. A written test on the unit should, then, be based on these terms.

banner	jewelry
cast	kiln
center of interest	loom
coil	medium
collage	mold
creative	nearika
embroidery	nonfunctional
fire	pendant
folk art	pennant
functional	score
glaze	sequin
slip	three-dimensional
stitchery	warp
symbol	weaving
tapestry	weft
textile	woven
texture	yarn

Skills

The artworks students create in this unit should meet the standards listed below. Be certain that the students are aware of these standards both as they plan and as they work. You may choose to keep the list posted throughout the time spent on this unit.
Pottery:
- The clay pieces are smoothly joined together.

Crafts:
- The artwork reflects a well-planned design.
- The symbols used for communication are effective.

Textiles:
- There is variety in the materials, colors, and patterns used.

Applications of Knowledge

Listening to a student talk about an artwork can give you a true sense of how much the student understands the basic elements and principles of design. However, the planning behind such a discussion is important. First, the work to be discussed must be chosen in advance and studied by the teacher. Questions must be written that will lead the student into the correct areas of emphasis. Last, the discussion should be arranged to take place on a one-to-one basis so that the more reticent students are not left out of a group discussion.

A suggested artwork to use for discussion purposes in this unit is the beautiful and colorful modern tapestry by Helena Hernmarck entitled *Sailing*.

Supplementary Materials and Resources

Nigrosh, Leon I. *Claywork—Form and Idea in Ceramic Design.* Worcester, Mass.: Davis Publications, Inc., 1984.

This standard, comprehensive, easy-to-use guide for working with clay provides detailed coverage to answer the needs of students and teachers involved in ceramics. Forming, throwing, and coiling techniques are discussed together with suggestions for decoration techniques. This is a comprehensive reference book to keep in the classroom.

North American Indian. Modesto, Calif.: Nasco Arts and Crafts, 1984. Slides.

This is a comprehensive survey of the Indian arts of North America from Alaska to Mexico. It illustrates the way of life, social structure, and environment of each Indian group, and shows their different forms of art.

Rainey, Sanita R. *Weaving Without a Loom.* Worcester, Mass.: Davis Publications, Inc., 1984.

This book is a good introduction to weaving. It stresses that there is no need for a loom, encouraging the students to use fingers, cardboard, wire mesh, burlap, paper, objects from nature, etc., to explore the versatile craft of weaving. The book also explains design basics, the use of colors, line and space organization, and how to express an idea or mood through simple two- and three-dimensional weaving.

TEACHING SUGGESTIONS for Lessons 71–82

LESSON 71

Clay Coil Pottery

Suggested Art Materials

See the art materials list in the student book.

Planning Ahead

To make sure the clay is in a workable condition, keep each student's portion wrapped in an airtight plastic bag until it is time for the lesson. The bags can then be used to store any incomplete pieces between lessons.
Additional Materials Needed:
small plastic bags

Helpful Teaching Hints

• Demonstrate how to make a coil, stressing that creating an even coil requires equal pressure by the hands.
• Supervise the students when they are joining the coils, as failure at this point can be frustrating.
• See Lesson 63 for further information on drying, glazing, and firing clay.

Safety Precautions

When using sharp tools, always cut *away* from the body and keep fingers out of the path. If the pottery is to be fired, do not move within two feet of the kiln until it has completely cooled.

Book Strand

Book strand 16, Being a Designer, includes this lesson in its diagram, pictured at the top of the next column. See page xvi for a complete description of this strand.

Being a Designer

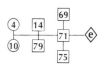

LESSON 72

Fancy Pots

Suggested Art Materials

See the art materials list for this lesson in the student book.

Planning Ahead

Roll and cut the day slabs beforehand, storing them individually in plastic bags.

Helpful Teaching Hints

• Air bubbles caused by rolling and working the clay can be pricked with any sharp instrument to prevent their damaging the pots during firing.
• See Lesson 63 for further information on drying, firing, and glazing clay.

Safety Precautions

When using sharp tools, always cut *away* from the body and keep fingers out of the path. If the pottery is to be fired, do not move within two feet of the kiln until it has completely cooled.

Book Strands

Book strand 4, Art with Flat Planes, and book strand 7, Exploring Textures, include this lesson in their diagrams, pictured below. See page xiv for complete descriptions of these strands.

Art with Flat Planes   Exploring Textures

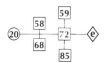   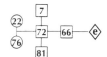

LESSON 73

Creative Mask-making

Suggested Art Materials

See the art materials list for this lesson in the student book.

Helpful Teaching Hints

- Discuss various masks the students have worn or seen. Refer to the masks in the text as you point out the use of exaggeration for dramatic effect in the making of masks.
- Have the students spend as much time as they want on the preliminary sketches. Students usually do a better job on projects of this nature if they know what they are going to do before beginning the actual work.
- Have the students immediately clean (with paint thinner) the brushes used for shallac. Students should consistently be taught how to properly care for art materials.

Safety Precautions

Use glue, shellac, and paint thinner only in a well-ventilated area. When using sharp tools, always cut *away* from the body and keep fingers out of the path.

Book Strand

Book strand 5, Faces and Feelings, includes this lesson in its diagram, pictured below. See page xiv for a complete description of this strand.

Faces and Feelings

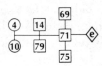

LESSON 74

Helmets, Hats, and Headdresses

Suggested Art Materials

See the art materials list for this lesson in the student book.

Planning Ahead

Collect party hats to use in this lesson.

Helpful Teaching Hints

- Since paper party hats are usually simply constructed, students can better understand what to do in this lesson after examining such hats. If possible, take one of the hats apart, discussing step-by-step how the designer created it.
- Again, allow the students plenty of time to draw sketches of their hats.

Book Strand

Book strand 14, From Observation to Imagination, includes this lesson in its diagram, pictured below. See page xv for a complete description of this strand.

From Observation to Imagination

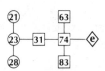

LESSON 75

Inexpensive Jewelry

Suggested Art Materials

See the art materials list for this lesson in the student book.

Helpful Teaching Hints

- Bring in examples of inexpensive costume jewelry. Explain that much of this kind of jewelry consists totally of man-made materials.*
- After the students have created their jewelry, suggest that they create a special class collage using the pieces. The effect of many small, shiny, three-dimensional pieces composing a unified design is quite striking against a black background.**

Additional Materials Needed:
  * costume jewelry
 ** large piece of plywood or heavy cardboard, comparably-sized piece of black velvet or other material, staple gun

Safety Precautions

Use glue, shellac, and paint thinner only in a well-ventilated area.

Book Strand

Book strand 16, Being a Designer, includes this lesson in its strand, pictured below. See page xvi for a complete description of this strand.

Being a Designer

LESSON 76

A Picture to See and Touch

Suggested Art Materials

See the art materials list in the student book.

Planning Ahead

Tell the students in advance to collect scraps of materials from anyone who sews in their families. Additionally, you should get swatches from fabric stores, upholsterers, or interior designers.
Additional Materials Needed:
scraps of fabric

Helpful Teaching Hints

Relate this lesson to other forms of picture composition. Talk about the importance of the center of interest, balance, arrangement, and textural and tactile effects for a textile collage.

Book Strand

Book strand 7, Exploring Textures, includes this lesson in its diagram, pictured below. See page xiv for a complete description of this strand.

Exploring Textures

LESSON 77

Folk Art Yarn Pictures

Suggested Art Materials

See the art materials list in the student book.

Helpful Teaching Hints

Use this lesson to stress the important design principle of unity.
• Unity is found in the use of a single type of material.
• Unity is created by using one color for outlining.

Book Strand

Book strand 6, Enjoying Color, includes this lesson in its diagram, pictured below. See page xiv for a complete description of this strand.

Enjoying Color

LESSON 78

Pennants, Flags, and Banners

Teaching suggestions for this lesson and for Lesson 79 follow.

LESSON 79

Badges and Patches

Suggested Art Materials

See the art materials lists for these lessons in the student book.

Planning Ahead

Collect samples and pictures of these art forms, since symbols and signs are abstract ideas best explained through the use of concrete samples.
Additional Materials Needed:
examples or pictures of the art forms featured in these lessons

Helpful Teaching Hints

• Have the students suggest some symbols they have noticed.
• Name some ideas and have the students suggest representative signs or symbols, and vice versa.

Book Strands

Book strand 1, Thinking with Contours, and book strand 16, Being a Designer, include Lesson 78 in their diagrams, pictured below. See pages xiii and xvi, respectively, for a complete description of these strands.

Thinking with Contours   Being a Designer

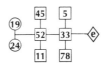   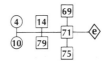

LESSON 80

Creating with Stitches

Suggested Art Materials

See the art materials list for this lesson in the student book.

Helpful Teaching Hints

- Define the terms *embroidery, stitchery, tapestry, fibers,* and *appliqué* for your students. Show samples or pictures of each type of needlework.*
- Encourage your students to be imaginative with their designs. Point out that bold stitches and colors work best for dynamic designs, while pastel colors and petite stitches complement intricate designs.

Additional Materials Needed:
* examples or pictures of needlework designs

Safety Precautions

Ask the students to be careful with needles, pulling them away from face and body. Make sure needles are stored in the correct place.

Book Strands

Book strand 2, Abstract Puzzles, and book strand 8, Studying Lines, include this lesson in their diagrams, pictured below. See pages xiii and xiv, respectively, for complete descriptions of these strands.

Abstract Puzzles   Studying Lines

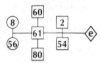 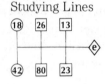

LESSON 81

Flat Loom Weaving

Suggested Art Materials

See the art materials list for this lesson in the student book.

Helpful Teaching Hints

- Bring in an example of a loosely woven piece of cloth. Let the students examine the sample to actually see the warp and the weft and how they are worked into the design.*
- Encourage the students to think of unusual uses for their cloths or unusual ways to display them.

Additional Materials Needed:
* sample of woven cloth

Safety Precautions

Remind the students of the two rules for using X-acto knives:
(1) Cut *away* from the body.
(2) Keep fingers out of the cutting path.

Book Strand

Book strand 7, Exploring Textures, includes this lesson in its diagram, pictured at the top of the next column. See page xiv for a complete description of this strand.

Exploring Textures

LESSON 82

American Indian Art

Suggested Art Materials

See the art materials list for this lesson in the student book.

Helpful Teaching Hints

- Collect examples and pictures of Indian artwork to display for the students' benefit. Discuss the colors used and the meanings of some of the signs and symbols. (Encyclopedias are good resources for this information.) Encourage the students to create their own meaningful symbols.*
- Have brown paper on hand for students who want to create artworks resembling buffalo hides. They can depict their designs on the brown paper and then stain the edges using cotton dipped in thin brown or black paint.**
- Tell the students to take plenty of time in the planning stage.

Additional Materials Needed:
 * examples of Indian artwork
** brown paper, cotton, brown or black paint

Book Strand

Book strand 10, Ideas from Other Cultures, and book strand 21, Artists and Art Styles, include this lesson in their diagrams, pictured below. See pages xv and xviii, respectively, for a complete description of these strands.

Ideas from Other Cultures   Artists and Art Styles

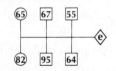 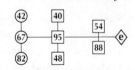

Exploring Art
The Winter Count

See page 47 for an explanation and teaching suggestions.

Unit VI
Expressing Feelings and Imagination

Learning Objectives

In this unit, the students will achieve the following objectives:

Understanding Art

- Understand new art terms used to label styles and types of art
- Understand the roles of imagination and feelings in creating and appreciating art

Creating Art

- Create a variety of art projects, using different media and techniques, to express emotions and ideas
- Develop an individual style, based on experimentation and exposure to numerous artworks, and adaptable to different assignments
- Produce artwork that creatively expresses verbal messages

Appreciating Art

- Discuss how well-known artists use a variety of media and styles to convey feelings and ideas
- See art as a creative outlet for their own expressions of emotions and imagination

Unit Strands

A strand consists of a group of related lessons where the student is expected to begin with one of the lesson choices available on the far left (arranged vertically), complete it, proceed horizontally to the next group of choices, make a choice and complete the lesson, and so forth, until the entire sequence has been completed. (See page v for complete instructions on using strands.) The unit strands for this unit are diagrammed at the top of the next column.

Strand M: Imagineering

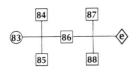

Strand N: Expressive Arts

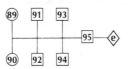

Background Information

This unit's lessons are designed to stimulate students' imaginations and encourage them to creatively express their feelings and ideas. It offers them opportunities to discover their own emerging artistic directions while exploring various art forms, the styles of recognized artists, and a variety of media.

Lessons 83, 84, and 85 invite students to picture their dreams, wishes, and fantasies as imaginatively as possible. A wide range of media is available to the students for each project. This facilitates free expression of ideas and feelings.

Lessons 86 and 87 introduce the craft of story illustration, as exemplified in storybooks and comic books. By illustrating materials they enjoy and are familiar with, students learn to project their imaginations verbally and visually. The verbal/visual connection is continued in Lesson 88, Splat! Bonk! Varoom!, where students learn that words can be symbolically represented.

Lesson 89, Surprise and Fun in Art, reminds us that most artists retain a childlike sense of wonder and an imaginative way of viewing the world all their lives. Students should be aware that while a number of artists share a sense of humor with us in their major works, others confine their whimsical sides to their private sketchbooks. Learning to share a sense of humor through art strengthens a student's confidence in the validity of his or her view of the world.

Lesson 90, The Eyes Have It, and Lesson 94, The Sun as a Symbol, are similar in that they focus on the use of symbols in art. Both lessons can be enriched by incorporating art history, mythology, poetry, and illustration.

Lesson 91, A Feeling of Peace, and Lesson 92, Feelings That Are Opposite, explore the expression of feelings and/or ideas as symbols in art. As in many of the previous lessons, a good rapport with your students is needed so you can guide them in discussions about their feelings and beliefs, and talk with them about how they want to depict them.

Lesson 95, Mexican Influence on Art, shows the students how the art of Mexico has influenced Mexican-American artists. By creating paintings or objects, using Mexican motifs, the students learn to appreciate the cultural backgrounds of other peoples.

Strategies for Motivation

The point of this unit is to encourage the students to use their imaginations. To help free their creativity, there is much emphasis on examining and verbalizing emotions and ideas. The following suggestions will further encourage creativity and imagination.

• Discuss and list on the board the students' dreams, wishes, and fantasies, so they can see that most people have similar ones.
• Read a passage from *Lord of the Rings* or another fantasy tale; have the students visualize the characters in the story and then verbally describe them using vivid details.
• Play a recording of a story and ask the students to draw or paint a picture of it while listening.
• Invite a local newspaper cartoonist or an illustrator to demonstrate his or her techniques.
• Invite a mime to act out a story showing many different emotions.
• Invite a Mexican-American artist or craftsperson (or an artist of another ethnic background) to demonstrate and discuss his or her work.

Extending Art

Exploring Art

The Exploring Art feature in Unit VI links art skills with study skills and Latin American history, directing the students to research the work of Mexico's historical muralists José Clemente Orozco and Diego Rivera. The feature then guides the students in creating their own murals that reflect the Mexican muralists' style. Introduce the students to the Art Reference and Art History sections of the library; in addition, make the student aware of local murals, either in the school or in other civic buildings. Encourage the students to work on their murals in groups of three to five. Specific extensions of this feature could include the following:

• Suggest varied media for student murals. Mosaic tiles and bas-relief sculpture, as well as paint and pastel, are possibilities.

• Allow the students to research the history of your school, community, or state, either by reading and visiting museums or by interviewing older people, and to choose mural themes based on their findings.

Additional Activities

The following activities may be used to enhance the lessons in this unit. (See the individual lesson guides for specific applications.)

• As a class, paint a mural of storybook characters for the school library or a day-care center.
• Have the students develop comic strips for the school paper.
• Ask the students to write short poems or stories and illustrate them.
• Let students paint a "trompe l'oeil" ("fool the eye") panel in the classroom. (example: a door where there isn't one)
• Have a Mexican fiesta, displaying Mexican-inspired artwork, serving Mexican food, playing Mexican music, etc.
• Exhibit various story illustrations, comic books, and examples of Pop art, identifying them as valid art forms.

Evaluating Procedures

As noted in the introduction to this book, evaluation in art classes poses unique problems for the teacher. (See pages vi-vii.) The Learning Outcomes address the need for self-evaluation and tests the students on the details of what they have learned. However, the teacher still needs some means of determing the extent of a student's application of specifics to a solid core of basic art knowledge. Three things are involved in this type of evaluation:

1. A written test of the student's recall of important facts
2. An examination of the student's artwork in terms of the achievement of certain previously stated goals
3. An oral discussion with the student involving his or her comments on a particular piece of art

These three evaluative components for Unit VI are explained below.

Vocabulary

Students who complete this unit should be able to define and correctly use the art terms listed below. A written test on the unit should, then, be based on these terms.

abstract
Baroque
caricature
cartoon art
cartoonist
centaur
collage
concrete poetry
creative
distort

fantasy
frame
illustrator
media
mural
mythical
narrative
Pop art
style
symbol

Skills

The artworks students create in this unit should meet the standards listed below. Be certain that the students are aware of these standards both as they plan and as they work. You may choose to keep the list posted throughout the time spent on this unit.

• The artwork communicates a definite message or feeling.
• The artist's personal style is evident.
• The artwork is symbolic, functioning on a level above that which is merely seen.

Application of Knowledge

Listening to a student talk about an artwork can give you a true sense of how much the student understands the basic elements and principles of design. However, the planning behind such a discussion is important. First, the work to be discussed must be chosen in advance and studied by the teacher. Questions must be written that will lead the student into the correct areas of emphasis. Last, the discussion should be arranged to take place on a one-to-one basis so that the more reticent students are not left out of a group discussion.

A suggested artwork to use for discussion purposes in this unit is the fanciful and symbolic painting by Jean-Léon Gérôme entitled *The Two Majesties*.

Supplementary Materials and Resources

Teacher Resources

Feiffer, Jules. *The Great Comic Book Heroes*. New York: The Dial Press, 1965.
This book discusses the historical, social, and artistic merit of comic book art. It includes color reproductions of original strips—Superman, Captain Marvel, Captain America, Wonder Woman, and others.

Gombrich, G.O. *The Art of Illusion*. Princeton, NJ: Princeton University Press, 1961.

This is a study in the psychology of pictorial representation. It covers distortion in art, bizarre perspective, and odd effects.

Gorey, Edward. *Amphigorey Also*. New York: Gongdon & Weed, Inc., 1983.
Gorey has a macabre sense of humor, but his animals in "The Utter Zoo Alphabet" and "The Sopping Thursday's" humor are applicable for this unit.

Gosling, Nigel. *Gustave Doré*. New York: Praeger Publishers, Inc., 1974.
Many of these black-and-white prints show Doré's sense of adventure, fun, and fantasy. A skilled illustrator, he depicts social life, fantastic monsters, and mysterious castles with equal ease. The pictures are accompanied by text.

Hathaway, Nancy. *The Unicorn*. New York: Viking Press, 1980.
This book covers the history of the unicorn as a mythological creature. Numerous drawings and art works showing the unicorn and other beasts are included, many in color.

Klein, H. Arthur. *Graphic Worlds of Peter Brueghel the Elder*. New York: Dover Publications, Inc., 1963.
This book includes black-and-white prints of Brueghel's drawings and etchings. Many of his more bizarre works are included, so you will want to select the most appropriate pieces. The text accompanying the pictures is scholarly in nature.

Student Resources

Hergé. *The Adventures of Tintin*. Boston: Atlantic, Little, Brown, 1974.
This is the famous book, translated from French, about Tintin and his dog Snowy—their travels and adventures all over the world. It is a large format, paperbacked comic book with a fast-moving story line and good color illustrations.

Lee, Alan and David Day. *Castles*. Toronto: Bantam Books, 1984.
Elegantly illustrated with drawings by Lee, Day's text describes the myths, romance, and fantasy connected with castles.

Lee, Stan and John Buscema. *How to Draw Comics the Marvel Way*. New York: Simon and Schuster, Inc., 1978.

This book shows the tools needed and gives instruction in basic perspective, action figure drawing, and developing a page and story line. The examples are all from the original Marvel comics and are black-and-white reproductions. The book is a paperback.

TEACHING SUGGESTIONS for Lessons 83–95

LESSON 83

Wishes and Daydreams

Suggested Art Materials

See the art materials list in the student book.

Planning Ahead

Collect and exhibit reproductions of artists which depict dream and fantasy worlds. Refer to the artists shown in the text, and include works by Klee, Chagall, Miró, and Bemelmans. Appropriate works by Breughel, Bosch, and Doré may also be used.
Additional Materials Needed:
reproductions by well-known artists which depict dream and fantasy worlds

Helpful Teaching Hints

- Encourage the students to use either a realistic or an abstract style and to try a variety of media.
- Stress that the students must look inward and really concentrate on their inner feelings in order to accurately portray them.

Book Strand

Book strand 14, From Observation to Imagination, includes this lesson in its diagram, pictured below. See page xv for a complete description of this strand.

From Observation to Imagination

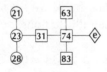

LESSON 84

Demons and Dragons

Suggested Art Materials

See the art materials list for this lesson in the student book.

Planning Ahead

Collect and display books with pictures of mythological beasts and creatures. As an alternative, arrange for the students to go to the library so they can do their own research.
Additional Materials Needed:
books with illustrations of mythological animals

Helpful Teaching Hints

- Exhibit pictures of mythological animals, and ask the students to identify as many animals as they can.
- Read aloud fairy tales or fantasy stories that describe fantastic animals.*
- Ask the students to bring to class their favorite books about fantasy animals to share with classmates.
Additional Materials Needed:
* fairy tales and fantasy books

Book Strand

Book strand 11, Imagineering, includes this lesson in its diagram, pictured below. See page xv for a complete description of this strand.

Imagineering

LESSON 85

Fantasy Tower

Suggested Art Materials

See the art materials list for this lesson in the student book.

Planning Ahead

Collect books with illustrations of towers: fairy tales, fantasy stories, science fiction, etc.
Additional Materials Needed:
books: fairy tales, fantasy stories, science fiction

Helpful Teaching Hints

- Explain the meaning of *fantasy* as something unreal that is invented in your imagination.
- Show pictures of towers as they have been depicted throughout the centuries—the Tower of Babel, the Tower of Pisa, etc.*

- Discuss the tower as a symbol of strength, and then ask the students what else a tower symbolizes.

Additional Materials Needed:
* pictures of famous towers

Book Strand

Book strand 4, Art with Flat Plates, includes this lesson in its diagram, pictured below. See page xiv for a complete description of this strand.

Art with Flat Planes

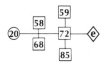

LESSON 86

Storytelling with Art

See Lesson 87 for teaching suggestions.

Related Art Career (book illustrator)

The book illustrator creates art to enhance or amplify the printed page. This career in applied arts is one of the closest to fine arts. In order to develop experience, contacts, and business knowledge, many illustrators begin their careers by working for an art service or group of illustrators who contract work with larger companies. Some illustrators prefer to work mostly on a free-lance basis.

Gather a collection of literature books for students to look through to learn about the different art styles of book illustrators. Discuss the various media, techniques, and art styles used.

If possible, invite an established book illustrator into the classroom to give a demonstration and discuss his or her artwork; or have students critique the work of an illustrator they like.

LESSON 87

Comic Art

Suggested Art Materials

See the art materials lists for these lessons in the student book.

Planning Ahead

Collect and exhibit well-illustrated children's story and comic books, and ask students to also bring in their favorites.

Additional Materials Needed:
illustrated storybooks, comic books

Helpful Teaching Hints

- Encourage the students to choose stories they are familiar with to illustrate.
- Read a favorite story (or passages) aloud, and ask the students to illustrate the parts they most enjoy.*
- Show that comic book art is considered a valid form of art by exhibiting Pop art by Warhol and other Pop artists.**
- Explain the meaning of *distortion* as the act of changing shapes to make them more interesting.

Additional Materials Needed:
* storybooks
** examples of Pop art

Related Art Career (cartoonist)

Cartooning is a specialized career which is built on the same educational base as that of illustrator. (See Lesson 23.) The cartoonist strives to develop a unique style that, when combined with the written word, will convey a message or make a point. Some cartoonists prefer to concentrate their art in specialized areas, such as witty humor, political satire, or adventure. In addition to creating cartoon art for the printed medium, the world of animation beckons some cartoonists to apply their art for television, videos, or movies. Specialized training and experience is necessary for this growing field.

Conduct a brainstorming session with students and list some of their favorite cartoon characters. If possible, have a collection of cartoon pictures on hand. Select several cartoon characters and discuss with students how the artists' particular art style has contributed to the creation of unique characters with definite personality traits. Identify some of the features of the characters and the styles of the artists who developed them.

Book Strands

Book strand 12, The Look of Distance, and book strand 17, The Quest for Self-Expression, include Lesson 86 in their diagrams, pictured below. See pages xv and xvi, respectively, for complete descriptions of these strands.

The Look of Distance

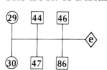

The Quest for Self-Expression

Book strand 5, Faces and Feelings, includes Lesson 87 in its diagram, pictured below. See page xiv for a complete description of this strand.

Faces and Feelings

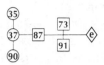

LESSON 88

Splat! Bonk! Varoom!

Suggested Art Materials

See the art materials list for this lesson in the student book.

Planning Ahead

Collect, or have students collect, examples of words which illustrate a sound (from magazines, newspapers, or comics). Also collect examples of onomatopoetic poems to read aloud.
Additional Materials Needed:
examples of words illustrating sounds, poems using onomatopoetic words

Helpful Teaching Hints

• Read aloud poems featuring onomatopoetic words. Ask the students to illustrate these poems.
• Show examples from comic strips, cartoons, and comic books to illustrate the lesson.*
• Show examples of Pop art.**
Additional Materials Needed:
  * comic strips, cartoons, and comic books
** examples of Pop art

Book Strand

Book strand 15, All About People, includes this lesson in its diagram, pictured below. See page xvi for a complete description of this strand.

All About People

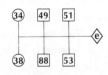

LESSON 89

Surprise and Fun in Art

Suggested Art Materials

See the art materials list for this lesson in the student book.

Planning Ahead

Collect reproductions by Hogarth, Piranesi, and Escher which show odd approaches to perspective. If possible, find trompe l'oeil (fool the eye) paintings and examples of anamorphic art (must be viewed from an angle, or in a mirror, to appear correct).
Additional Materials Needed:
reproductions of works by Hogarth, Piranesi, Escher, and others.

Helpful Teaching Hints

• Show slides or reproductions of works by the artists mentioned above.
• Point out that some artists specialize in doing these kinds of puzzles, that that is all they are known for, while others do it only occasionally, for fun.

Book Strand

Book strand 13, Artistic Surprises, includes this lesson in its diagram, pictured below. See page xv for a complete description of this strand.

Artistic Surprises

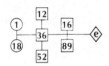

LESSON 90

The Eyes Have It

Teaching suggestions for this lesson and for Lesson 94 follow.

Suggested Art Materials

See the art materials lists for these lessons in the student book.

Planning Ahead

• Plan on teaching Lesson 90 and Lesson 94 together, since the symbolism of eyes and the sun is similar.
• Find, or have the students find, pictures emphasizing eyes and the sun. Include reproductions of works by well-known painters and craftspersons in your collection.*
Additional Materials Needed:
* pictures emphasizing eyes and the sun, reproductions by painters (Picasso and Matisse for eyes, Van Gogh for the sun)

Helpful Teaching Hints

• Point out that the eyes and the sun have been used as symbols in art for thousands of years and that

they are recognized from culture to culture, although the precise meanings might differ.
- Read stories and poems about eyes and the sun; ask the students to illustrate them.*

Additional Materials Needed:
* stories and poems featuring eyes, sun (check folklore sources for Native American myths and poems)

Book Strands

Book strand 5, Faces and Feelings, and book strand 3, Artistic Visions, include Lesson 90 in their diagrams, pictured below. See page xiv for a complete description of these strands.

Faces and Feelings   Artistic Visions

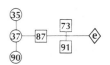   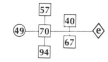

LESSON 91

A Feeling of Peace

Suggested Art Materials

See the art materials list for this lesson in the student book.

Planning Ahead

Collect pictures that depict peace. Be prepared to discuss with the students their feelings about peace. Have them come up with visuals that demonstrate these feelings.
Additional Materials Needed:
pictures depicting peace

Helpful Teaching Hints

- Have the students design posters about peace.
- Ask the students to write out their definitions of peace and then illustrate them.

Book Strand

Book strand 5, Faces and Feelings, includes this lesson in its diagram, pictured below. See page xiv for a complete description of this strand.

Faces and Feelings

```
      (35)
              73
(37)─ 87 ─        ─◇e
              91
      (90)
```

LESSON 92

Feelings That Are Opposite

Suggested Art Materials

See the art materials list for this lesson in the student book.

Planning Ahead

You may want to collect additional pictures and reproductions that show opposite feelings and ideas, or show slides.
Additional Materials Needed:
slides or pictures showing opposite feelings

Helpful Teaching Hints

- Divide the class in half. Have one half express one emotion while the other half expresses the opposite emotion. Then switch their roles.
- Ask the students to list all the things they like and dislike, love and hate. Then have them choose the most important thing and illustrate them.

Book Strand

Book strand 11, Imagineering, includes this lesson in its diagram, pictured below. See page xv for a complete description of this strand.

Imagineering

```
          16
 (9)
     53 ─ 92 ─◇e
(41)
          84
```

LESSON 93

The Original You

Suggested Art Materials

See the art materials list for this lesson in the student book.

Planning Ahead

Collect slides and prints of artwork, including three-dimensional work, so the students will have enough to choose from and emulate. If you are offering a wide range of media for students to choose from, be sure to have ample materials on hand.
Additional Materials Needed:
slides and reproductions of a variety of artwork

Helpful Teaching Hints

- Talk with students individually, to help each decide what his or her style is.
- Have the students do rough sketches first, indicating the media they intend to use.
- Have the students using similar media work in the same area.

Book Strand

Book strand 17, The Quest for Self-Expression, includes this lesson in its strand, pictured on the following page. See page xvi for a complete description of this strand.

The Quest for Self Expression

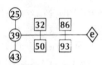

LESSON 94

The Sun as a Symbol

Suggested Art Materials

See the art materials lists for these lessons in the student book.

Planning Ahead

- Plan on teaching Lesson 90 and Lesson 94 together, since the symbolism of eyes and the sun is similar.
- Find, or have the students find, pictures emphasizing eyes and the sun. Include reproductions of works by well-known painters and craftspersons in your collection.*

Additional Materials Needed:

* pictures emphasizing eyes and the sun, reproductions by painters (Picasso and Matisse for eyes, Van Gogh for the sun)

Helpful Teaching Hints

- Point out that the eyes and the sun have been used as symbols in art for thousands of years and that they are recognized from culture to culture, although the precise meanings might differ.
- Read stories and poems about eyes and the sun; ask the students to illustrate them.*

Additional Materials Needed:

* stories and poems featuring eyes, sun (check folklore sources for Native American myths and poems)

Book Strands

Book strand 5, Faces and Feelings, and book strand 3, Artistic Visions, include Lesson 90 in their diagrams, pictured below. See page xiv for a complete description of these strands.

Faces and Feelings   Artistic Visions

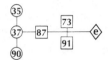   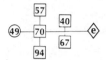

LESSON 95

Mexican Influences on Art

Suggested Art Materials

See the art materials list for this lesson in the student book.

Planning Ahead

Gather examples of Mexican art and artifacts.

Helpful Teaching Hints

- Ask Mexican-American students to talk about their culture and bring examples of artwork to share. (Extend this invitation to students of other cultural backgrounds as well.)
- Invite a Mexican-American artist or craftsperson to talk about his or her art.

Book Strand

Book strand 10, Ideas from Other Cultures, includes this lesson in its diagram, pictured below. See page xv for a complete description of this strand.

Ideas from Other Cultures

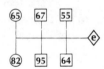

Exploring Art
Creating a Wall Mural

See page 54 for an explanation and teaching suggestions.

SUPPLIES CHART*

Supplies/Lesson Number	1	2	3	4	5	6	7	8	9	10	11	12	13	14	15	16	17	18	19	20	21	22	23	24	25	26	27
Bowls																											
Boxes (various sizes)																											
Brayer									●	●		●															
Brushes							●	●	●	●	●					●	●								●		
Calligraphy tools													●														
Candles (white)																											
Cardboard	●			●		●				●							●										
Carving tools																											
Chalk																											
Clay																											
Cloth																											
Colored construction paper		●	●																							●	
Colored markers				●										●	●	●		●						●			
Colored pencils														●										●			
Crayons				●										●		●		●							●		
Cutting tools												●															
Drawing instruments																											
Glue	●	●	●	●	●					●																	●
Ink (black)			●										●														
Knife											●																
Linoleum block												●															
Magazines with pictures																											●
Miscellaneous objects	●							●	●										●	●	●	●		●	●		
Mixing tray							●	●	●	●	●					●	●								●		
Natural objects						●	●																●				
Oil pastels				●																						●	
Paint thinner																											
Papier-mâché																											
Pens														●	●		●								●		
Plaster of paris																											
Popsicle sticks																											
Printing ink								●	●	●		●															
Rolling pin																											
Root vegetables											●																
Ruler											●		●	●			●										
Sand																											
Scissors	●	●		●	●	●			●	●																●	●
Shellac																											
Stapler																											
String										●																	
Stitching materials																											
Tape																			●								
Tapestry needle																											
Tempera paint							●	●	●	●	●					●	●								●		
Tissue paper			●	●																							
Turpentine																										●	
Vinegar																											
Watercolor paints																											
Wood strips																											
X-acto knife				●																							

*The following items are needed in nearly every lesson, and so are not included on the chart: pencil and eraser, white drawing or sketching paper, newspaper, water, and paper towels. Also notice that Lessons 83-95 (Unit VI) are not represented. These lessons instruct students to choose their own art materials.

Supplies/Lesson Number	28	29	30	31	32	33	34	35	36	37	38	39	40	41	42	43	44	45	46	47	48	49	50	51	52	53	54
Bowls					F							F	F														
Boxes (various sizes)					R							R	R														
Brayer					E							E	E														
Brushes				•	E							E	E	•	•	•	•	•	•	•	•	•	•	•	•	•	•
Calligraphy tools																											
Candles (white)					C							C	C			•											
Cardboard					H							H	H						•								
Carving tools					O							O	O														
Chalk	•				I							I	I														
Clay					C							C	C														
Cloth					E							E	E														
Colored construction paper																				•							
Colored markers				•					•					•													
Colored pencils																											
Crayons				•					•							•											
Cutting tools																											
Drawing instruments																									•		
Glue		•					•																				
Ink (black)																											
Knife																											
Linoleum block																											
Magazines with pictures							•			•																	•
Miscellaneous objects																		•									
Mixing tray					•									•	•	•	•	•	•	•	•	•	•	•	•	•	•
Natural objects																											
Oil pastels				•					•																		
Paint thinner																											
Papier-mâché																											
Pens																•											
Plaster of paris																											
Popsicle sticks																											
Printing ink																											
Rolling pin																											
Root vegetables																											
Ruler	•								•			•	•						•								
Sand																											
Scissors		•					•		•										•								
Shellac																											
Stapler																											
String																											
Stitching materials																											
Tape																	•		•								
Tapestry needle																											
Tempera paint				•											•					•				•	•	•	•
Tissue paper																											
Turpentine																											
Vinegar																											
Watercolor paints														•		•	•	•	•	•	•	•	•	•			
Wood strips																											
X-acto knife																											

Supplies/Lesson Number	55	56	57	58	59	60	61	62	63	64	65	66	67	68	69	70	71	72	73	74	75	76	77	78	79	80	81	82
Bowls							●	●		●							●	●			●							F
Boxes (various sizes)								●								●												R
Brayer																												E
Brushes	●									●					●	●				●	●							E
Calligraphy tools																												
Candles (white)																												C
Cardboard				●	●										●		●		●	●		●	●				●	H
Carving tools									●	●	●		●	●														O
Chalk														●												●		I
Clay									●	●	●		●	●														C
Cloth								●							●			●	●			●				●		E
Colored construction paper																								●	●			
Colored markers						●									●					●					●			
Colored pencils																												
Crayons															●					●					●			
Cutting tools												●																
Drawing instruments																												
Glue		●	●	●	●	●									●	●		●	●	●	●	●	●	●				
Ink (black)																												
Knife									●	●	●																	
Linoleum block																												
Magazines with pictures																												
Miscellaneous objects		●				●		●				●						●	●	●								
Mixing tray	●									●					●	●				●	●							
Natural objects			●																									
Oil pastels																												
Paint thinner										●							●			●								
Papier-mâché																	●											
Pens							●	●	●																			
Plaster of paris							●	●	●																			
Popsicle sticks																	●	●										
Printing ink																												
Rolling pin											●			●			●											
Root vegetables																												
Ruler				●	●																						●	
Sand								●																				
Scissors		●	●	●	●										●	●		●		●	●	●	●	●	●	●	●	
Shellac										●		●						●		●								
Stapler				●	●														●									
String		●						●								●		●		●		●						
Stitching materials																										●	●	
Tape		●		●	●	●									●	●											●	
Tapestry needle																										●	●	
Tempera paint	●									●					●	●				●	●							
Tissue paper																												
Turpentine																												
Vinegar														●			●	●										
Watercolor paints	●																											
Wood strips														●			●											
X-acto knife				●											●				●									

63